One Step in a Poppy Field

One Step in a Poppy Field

The Inspirational Story of Lance Corporal Cayle Royce MBE

Bronwyn Royce

Pen & Sword

MILITARY

AN IMPRINT OF PEN & SWORD BOOKS LTD.
YORKSHIRE – PHILADELPHIA

First published in Great Britain in 2023
by Pen & Sword Military
An imprint of
Pen & Sword Books Limited
Yorkshire - Philadelphia

ISBN 978 1 39905 736 3

Typeset in INDIA by IMPEC eSolutions
Printed and bound in England by CPI Group (UK) Ltd, Croydon, CR0 4YY

Pen & Sword Books Ltd. incorporates the Imprints of Pen & Sword
Archaeology, Atlas, Aviation, Battleground, Discovery, Family History, History,
Maritime, Military, Naval, Politics, Railways, Select, Transport, True Crime,
Fiction, Frontline Books, Leo Cooper, Praetorian Press, Seaforth Publishing,
Wharncliffe, White Owl and After the Battle.

For a complete list of Pen & Sword titles please contact

PEN & SWORD BOOKS LIMITED
47 Church Street, Barnsley, South Yorkshire S70 2AS, United Kingdom
E-mail: enquiries@pen-and-sword.co.uk
Website: www.pen-and-sword.co.uk

Or

PEN AND SWORD BOOKS
1950 Lawrence Rd, Havertown, PA 19083, USA
E-mail: Uspen-and-sword@casematepublishers.com
Website: www.penandswordbooks.com

Praise for One Step in a Poppy Field

General The Lord Dannatt GCB CBE MC DL
Chief of the General Staff 2006-2009
Army President, The Not Forgotten

"Told from a mother's perspective, this book is a powerful testament to one woman's love and hope and to a son's determination and hope. The combination is electrifying, uplifting and deeply moving. Yes, the story starts in Afghanistan but it is as open-ended as Cayle's life and his achievements continue to be an inspiration to all who meet him or read this book."

Marshal of the Royal Air Force, The Lord Stirrup, KG, GCB, AFC, FRAeS, FCMI
Chief of the Defence Staff 2006-2010

"Courage comes in many forms. Commonly we think of single acts of daring performed in the face of obvious and imminent danger, but this is far from the whole picture. There is also the bravery required to face long-term pain and life-changing disability: to get up each morning knowing that every day will be a challenge; to muster the will and determination to do what used to be simple but is now a continual struggle; to accept that this is how things will be permanently. Then there is the bravery necessary to bear the suffering of a loved one: to sustain them through the dark times; to encourage and help them in their efforts to reconstruct their life; to support their search for purpose and joy. All of these forms of courage and more are at the heart of this book, from the battlefield to the hospital to rehabilitation and on to new and remarkable achievements. It is a story with an important message for us all: that bravery is praiseworthy in all its guises, but it is the every day acts of heroism that lead to the triumph of the human spirit."

The Rt Hon. The Lord Robathan PC
Parliamentary Under-Secretary of State for Welfare and Veterans
2010-2012
Minister of State for the Armed Forces 2012-2013

"The shocking injuries that Cayle received are sadly replicated among far too many soldiers who, as young men doing their duty, came home without limbs. When serving in the MOD, I saw how devastating these injuries could be, not just to the soldiers but also to the families – such as Cayle's mother – who together suffer the consequences of one step onto a hidden IED. We should honour these victims and never forget that sending young men into harm's way can have such terrible consequences, which is a lesson politicians need to learn."

General Sir Richard Barrons, KCB, CBE
Deputy Chief of the Defence Staff (Operations) 2011-2013
Commander, Joint Forces Command 2013-2016

"Everybody has regrets to manage at some time in their life. Very few, however, have to manage regret on the scale of stepping on a mine in Afghanistan, losing both legs and spending 48 days in a close-run battle for life. Cayle Royce has – and then he rebuilt his life brilliantly, rowing the Atlantic and flying a powered paraglider the length of the UK. His story puts what most of us call a challenge to shame, providing the perspective and inspiration to power through our own troubles. The example of sons like Cayle and mothers like Bronwyn makes the world a far better place for all of us."

Invictus
by William Ernest Henley

Out of the night that covers me,
Black as the pit from pole to pole,
I thank whatever gods may be
For my unconquerable soul.

In the fell clutch of circumstance
I have not winced nor cried aloud.
Under the bludgeonings of chance
My head is bloody, but unbowed.

Beyond this place of wrath and tears
Looms but the Horror of the shade,
And yet the menace of the years
Finds and shall find me unafraid.

It matters not how strait the gate,
How charged with punishments the scroll,
I am the master of my fate,
I am the captain of my soul.

Contents

It is now over 20 years since the beginning of the Afghanistan and Iraq Wars, and even longer since the end of the Second World War, the Korean War and the almost continuous operational deployments of the British military in the late Twentieth century. Many families and individuals are still living with the consequences of the loss of family members and life changing injuries in those operations and conflicts.

The Not Forgotten Association was founded in 1920 by US born Marta Cunningham after she discovered there were many thousands of wounded servicemen still under treatment, but who were lying in hospitals, often bored, lonely, and in severe pain. Cunningham established The Not Forgotten with the object of providing entertainment and recreation for those injured in war to alleviate the tedium of their lives and give them something to which they could look forward.

Today the NFA continues to support veterans and serving personnel alike who need their assistance. It supports an average of 10,000 beneficiaries each year, and since its founding estimates it has supported one million plus beneficiaries. In modern times however, they have also added respite breaks and challenge holidays to their services, so that younger and more ambitious veterans can boost their confidence and wellbeing.

Lance Corporal Cayle Royce is one of those veterans who is actively participating in Not Forgotten challenge events. This year he was a member of The Not Forgotten Association's 2,000km kayak expedition from Seattle to Skagway in Alaska. Known as the "Inside Passage" this follows one of the most forbidding coastlines in the world. Their aim was to encourage all veterans to achieve their personal goals and not to be limited by their injuries or trauma.

This book, although written from the perspective of his mother with contributions throughout from Cayle, shows the on-going battle injured veterans face. It is a book of how determination and hope, and the support of family and friends, can help overcome adversity. As the years pass it is important we still remember the ongoing impact on the lives of young men and women like Lance Corporal Royce, and the work of The Not Forgotten to support them.

Preface

"Where a bomb bursts on a distant plain, one might assume that the only impact – terrible though it undoubtedly is – would be on those in the immediate vicinity. Indeed through the decade of the most intense fighting of the war in Afghanistan the British public became used, even inured, to the sight of rows of hearses moving slowly through Royal Wootton Basset. Invariably these news stories would be accompanied by photos of the young men and women involved, frequently images taken while they were on operations. This only added to the feeling that this was a distant war affecting a new generation of Service personnel, yet another chapter of Kipling's Great Game. Of course the news was disturbing, of course we sympathised with those who had received life altering injuries or indeed had been killed, but still it remained surreal and somewhat removed from the mundanity of our day to day lives at home.

But what we did not understand is that the ripples from every explosion spread far, crossing borders and bridging cultures. They affect everyone associated with the individual who has the misfortune to be at the heart of the event. They change the life of each family beyond measure, they stun close-knit communities, and they require something special to mend. Just as elemental forces create life-altering wounds in the first instant, so something of similar power and intensity is required to fix them.

And so we come to Cayle Royce, his extraordinary mother Bronwyn, his brother Seth, his father Richard, and the community of which he is such an integral part.

The impact on Cayle Royce's family of that terrible day in 2012 was, of course, seismic. His home town of Dartmouth was also rocked to its core when one of their own was so grievously injured. There was an immediate feeling of helplessness, of disbelief, and of profound sympathy. But what no-one in the town knew, what none of us could possibly understand, was that this was not the tragic end of a story. It was the beginning of a tale of love, fortitude, and resolve that deserves to ring through the ages.

But this was no linear path to recovery, no Hollywood storyboard. This was a brutally tough journey that explored the limits of all involved, particularly the young man at the heart of it all. Cayle was surrounded by support and expertise, and yet in many ways he was totally alone. It would be him that found a way to rebuild his life, him that discovered a means of coming to terms with his catastrophic injuries, and him that emerged at the end of it all to achieve feats that were so Herculean that they bordered on the absurd. This book is the story of that journey, of the crushing lows and the soaring highs, but most of all his steadfast resolve to never, ever give up. Such resolve saw him defy overwhelming odds medically. Sometimes when basic physiology fails, all that is left is a crystal spirit. And sometimes that spirit will forge ahead regardless, dragging the shattered frame of a traumatised body along with it. So it proved with this most extraordinary young man.

The forces of war are powerful indeed, they scorch landscapes and shape nations. They harness the darkest elements of mankind's ability to maim and destroy, and they use it to swat aside life. But some forces are even stronger. In Bronwyn - his mother - Cayle had a champion who was steadfast, resolute, and utterly unwavering. She held the gaze of grim misfortune, stared it down, and took back her son.

There is a quote from Ralph Waldo Emerson that notes:

"Men are what their mothers made them."

Through the turbulence and the tides of the recovery process, Bronwyn was always there, and of course remains so to this day. She was so often a still point in his turning world, the rock around which his life swirled.

As a resident of Dartmouth, I have had the great fortune to cross paths with the family many times during Cayle's recovery. What was readily apparent was a collective will that brokered no compromise. They would get through this, the ties that bound them were simply too strong. And even through the dark early days after 2012, they would always make time for a chat, would enquire after the health of my own family, and brush aside my own queries and concerns. There was no self pity, and no railing against the vagaries of fate. There was, however, a job to do, and that was to be with Cayle throughout his journey however harrowing that journey may be. It was a matter of fact approach expressed with admirable brevity by Cayle himself in a BBC interview:

"My life has changed now – it's just a case of getting on with things."

But what was once the desperate straits of concern and grief for them both, has now become an overwhelming sense of purpose and pride. And this is because another chapter began. One where Cayle used the same inner spirit that had burned so brightly to aid his recovery, and turned it outwards towards a series of challenges. From modest beginnings – each a small victory in its own right – this ultimately led to the monumental feat of rowing 3,000 miles across the Atlantic in 48 days. That he did so as the skipper of a crew of amputees, four men with three legs between them, means that the crossing takes its place amongst the annals of any great athletic and exploratory achievement, from any age.

The last time I bumped into him was on the River Dart. I was kayaking downstream, going with the tide, when around the corner he appeared with another group of paddlers.

"Hey Monty" he said, and paddled over as the rest of his group moved on.

"Looking good Cayle!" I noted as he approached. And indeed he did - clear eyed, smiling, and strong. "And what are you up to?"

"Ah, you know, we're training to paddle the length of the Amazon, but Covid kind of got in the way of that. So we're looking at other options." He smiled and shrugged. "We'll figure it out I'm sure."

That last phrase could be his motto, a neat summation of who he is, what he has come through, and what he will go on to achieve.

And then he was gone, pushing on, doing the one thing he truly knows by forging ever onwards. Cayle Royce - head up, shoulders squared, and chin lifted. Paddling resolutely against the tide."

– Monty Halls

I put one foot on the bank, haul myself up behind Shorty, and step into the field.

There's no dramatic click or noise or sound or anything like that … it's just a BANG! I see the sky first and then a flash, like I'm swallowed by absolute darkness and blinding light at the same time. And then I hit the ground, hard and winded, my ears screaming and my heart pounding. There's no pain at first, but not for long. It slides over me like scalding oil. I try digging my heels into the soft earth so I can push myself into cover, but my left leg has gone and my right is hanging by a sinew. There's blood in my eyes. Has my hand gone too? The agony is suffocating.

I hear Shorty, who was blown onto his face by the force of the blast, shouting:

'Aaaah fuck. Is everyone all right?'

He staggers to his feet and runs over to me.

'Roll over mate, roll over. Listen to me, stay with me. You're going to be fine mate, you're going to be fine.'

I'm slipping away, but I can feel Jacko the medic tighten the tourniquets on the tatters of my legs. And I can hear their voices ordering me to live.

I am coming and going. I'm on a stretcher and the morphine is taking hold now. And then I hear someone chuckle. Have I just made a joke? I'm trying to think of something comforting – perhaps home – but my mind is clouding over. Then there's smoke. Blue smoke. It must be for the helicopter. I am being carried over rough ground. I can feel the bumps and the heat from the Chinook's engines blowing into my face. A glimpse of the evening sky and the dark inside the helicopter.

And then I'm given ketamine and I slide into a hole, the sound of the rotors following me down it. Whap, whap, whap.

1. Bell

Bronwyn
2 May 2012

The date was 2 May 2012 and remains forever etched in my mind. It was a day during which I felt my very core was being ripped from me. I was on the receiving end of news no mother wants to hear.

It was a Wednesday and I was feeling upbeat after a good day at work. The weather was beautifully clear, the air crisp as I headed for my daily 5 pm session at the local gym where I would meet up with a friend. Walking briskly along the embankment, I smiled to myself as I remembered the comment made by someone a few years earlier about me never just going for a walk – it always felt like a route march, a habit I had gotten into from walking with Cayle. To keep up with him, I stomped everywhere, my little legs moving faster than they should without physically breaking into a run. Stomping my way to the gym, I was reminded of the beauty of my surroundings in Dartmouth, the place I now called home. I gazed at the yachts and boats lazing on the sparkling river and once again reflected on the tranquillity of the setting. My thoughts rarely strayed far from my children and my two sons were on my mind. Both were serving in the British military – Cayle had deployed to Afghanistan with the Light Dragoons six weeks earlier; Seth, three years his junior, had recently joined the Royal Marines. Their childhoods and developing years in Cape Town, South Africa, played on my mind as I strode along the embankment. I considered, with motherly pride, their achievements and much of the joy I had experienced during their formative and young adult years. I also knew that they were now both doing what they loved.

In the ten minutes it took me to reach the gym my mood inexplicably altered. A sense of foreboding gripped me. Nevertheless, I signed myself in and entered the changing room to put on my bathing costume before making my way into the spa area.

'Come and join me in the pool and we can catch up,' Karon suggested enthusiastically.

Although hesitant and reluctant, I swam a few lengths before she asked,

'Are you okay? You don't seem to be your normal, bonkers self.'

I'm not sure whether I heard her the first time. The world was going on around me, but the voices that normally echoed around the pool were silenced. I had just one thing on my mind – I had to get home immediately.

'Bron! Are you okay?'

'Sorry Karon, I've had a great day,' I replied, 'but I need to be at home and I'm not sure why.'

'Come round to mine for dinner later then,' she said.

'I can't. Thank you, but I've really got to go. I feel like something might have happened. I need to be at home. I'll ring you.'

I had no idea then that Cayle had been injured, but I felt a sudden heaviness, a horrible sense of bad news on the horizon. And time slowed down with it. I showered, dressed and walked home as quickly as possible.

The flat I lived in was above an art framing shop on Anzac Street, a pretty little lane that leads up to old St Saviour's church. The flat overlooked the church square and it was in that square that I'd hugged Cayle goodbye a few weeks before.

'Don't worry, Mom,' he'd said. 'I'll be fine.'

The premonition was vague. Three days before Cayle was injured, I'd started organising my flat. I've always kept my home neat, but that Sunday was different. I went through all my drawers. Everything was taken out and refolded; I even colour-coded my underwear. I cleaned, vacuumed and polished everything. And then I went to the local shop and bought two AA batteries for the doorbell, which hadn't worked since I had moved into the flat.

* * *

When I turned the corner onto Anzac Street, it looked the same, as did my flat when I opened the door and stepped inside. But something was wrong. Once upstairs, I opened my laptop, turned on the television but muted it, and waited. I didn't know what was coming, I just knew I had to be there for it.

I remember the church bells ringing as Wednesday evenings are bell practice. During a lull in the chiming, the silence was shattered by the ringing of a different bell; my doorbell. My stomach lurched. The instant I heard that 'ding, dong', I knew it was about Cayle. Was he injured? Dead? I could only imagine the very worst.

I dragged myself up from the sofa and stumbled to the kitchen table. Motionless, I stood with one hand grasping the back of a wooden chair, the other gripping the door frame. Lying on the table were the dead AA batteries I had removed from the bell just three days before. The doorbell rang again, and then for a third time.

My heart was pounding as I stumbled down the stairs. The staircase leading down from the flat on the first floor to the front door was steep and narrow. The same stairs my boys had flown up and down during their constant comings and goings into and out of my home, never even mindful of the handrail I now gripped with everything in me to keep myself upright. I reached the last step; three feet in front of me was the cottage-paned glass door with two figures standing beyond it.

They were both men, in their forties and dressed in dark blue lounge suits, one man slightly taller than the other. They were surprisingly faceless, simply the anonymous bearers of bad news. Even now, there is no way I would be able to identify them in a line-up.

As I stood behind the glass, it was the taller man who held up his identification badge and spoke.

'Ms Royce? We are Casualty Notification Officers (CNOs). May we come in?'

I couldn't move. I could barely talk.

'Is he still alive?'

'Yes he is,' the tall man said. 'Now can you please open the door?'

I turned the latch, letting them in. My legs had gone to jelly and I had to hold onto the handrail to haul myself back up the flight of stairs.

In the sitting room, I sat on the edge of my sofa while they remained standing. I noticed that the taller man had a plain cardboard folder in his left hand. Within that folder were the details I was dreading.

'Is there someone you can call? Someone to come and sit with you?'

I couldn't think. Not because I didn't have friends who would support me, but because I don't like inconveniencing people.

'Thank you,' I said, 'but can you just tell me what has happened?'

The tall man first looked me straight in the eyes, then opened the folder and spoke:

'Your son, Cayle, was involved in an Improvised Explosive Device incident in Afghanistan at 18:06 Afghan time, 13:36 this afternoon UK time. One of his legs was instantly amputated and he's in surgery now in Camp Bastion, possibly having the other removed. He has other serious injuries and is in a critical state ... Ms Royce? Is there any other family?'

The voice brought me back to my living room. I had to call Seth. He was based in Beaconsfield, Buckinghamshire, doing a Pashto language course in preparation for his August deployment to Afghanistan. At the time of the call, he was sitting having coffee with a fellow Royal Marine in Starbucks. The phone rang twice.

'Mother dearest!'

I tried to speak, but the tears were streaming down my face and my voice choked with emotion. All I could say was,

'Sethy.'

He knew instantly that it was about Cayle.

'When is he coming home, Ma?'

There was no doubt in his question; he knew his older brother was going to make it home alive.

'He's been seriously injured, Sethy,' I said between sobs. 'I don't know what happens now but I will phone you later when I know more. Can you come home?'

'I'll be there as soon as I can, Ma. Love you.'

The CNOs made a call to the boys' father. Richard and I had divorced in 2010 and he was staying with a friend in France when he received the news. I later discovered that he was standing in the drive at the time, preparing his car for a road trip. On hearing the report, he had let out a cry and momentarily blacked out, before coming to and asking to speak to me.

'Oh Richard!' I wailed. 'Our beautiful boy.'

We cried down the phone line, parents together, united in this devastating moment of loss.

One of the CNOs informed me,

'Warrant Officer Armstrong will be here tomorrow at noon to fetch you and Seth and will drive you to QEHB.'

Queen Elizabeth Hospital Birmingham was the brand new medical facility to which Cayle would be transferred on his arrival in England.

'Oh, and we ask that for your own safety, no mention of this be put onto social media as unfortunately it could open the channels for abuse against you and your family. It may also attract a lot of media attention.'

There was clearly nothing more the CNOs could say or do.

'Our car is parked just around the corner,' the shorter man said.

'We will wait there for thirty minutes and if you need us, we'll come back. In the meantime, please ring someone and ask them to come and be with you until Seth gets here.'

He handed me his business card and with that, they let themselves out of my flat and were gone. I sat on the sofa and began to weep uncontrollably, from the very depths of my being. I had to do something but I was consumed by grief.

I phoned my oldest sister, Janice, in South Africa. She begged me to phone Karon, who lived on my street and who turned up at my front door minutes later, barefoot and breathless. We stood in the doorway and held each other for what felt like an eternity, as I told her the news between sobs. She led me upstairs to the sofa where I slumped down while she knelt in front of me, taking hold of the leg of my jeans.

'His life's over, Karon. My boy's life is over!'

'But he's not dead, Bron.'

'He's not dead but he's had his legs blown off. You don't understand. You don't know Cayle, his life will be over.'

Just then, an advert for the London Olympics came on the muted television. She turned to the screen then back to me.

'Oh, and soon we'll have the Paralympics for all the other fucking people whose lives are over. How over are their fucking lives? Have they given up? Cayle is still alive!'

It was as if she had slapped me across the face. I couldn't just cry. I couldn't give up. I needed to be Cayle's mother, I needed to be strong for him. I needed to love him, not mourn for him. I'd been there when Cayle had learned to walk for the first time. No matter how bad his injuries, I'd be there when he learned to do it all over again.

I phoned Janice to tell her that I was no longer alone, and then I turned to Karon.

'They're sending him home. They're going to send his stuff. They're going to send his boots. What good are his boots to him? Why are they going to send his boots home?' I sobbed.

As word got out around town, streams of people began messaging, some even arriving at the flat. Standing in the kitchen, Karon noticed the photograph stuck to my fridge of Cayle at about a year old wearing Richard's army boots. She thought how poignant it was and wondered whether to turn it face down.

The rest of the evening was a blur. People came and went and calls were made. Some I remember, others I don't. Cups of tea were brewed, most left undrunk. Seth arrived home moments before midnight. As the church bells chimed and all the other people melted away, I remember holding him – and the comfort it gave me – and then him tucking me into bed as if I were the child.

'I'll never be able to sleep, Sethy,' I protested, but he insisted. 'At least try to get some rest, Ma. Tomorrow is going to be a very long day.'

He kissed me on the top of my head and walked out of my bedroom.

As I lay my head on my pillow, I heard the front door close and I knew that Seth had gone out into the dark night to walk the streets.

In Cayle's wardrobe hung a black, down body warmer. It was one of the few things he had left behind; I got up out of my bed and put it on. It was far too big for me but I could smell my son's scent on it; wearing it gave me enormous comfort. 'We'll get through this,' I whispered. And then, as I lay back in bed, I realised that we would need the prayers and support of many. I sat up, unlocked my phone and wrote what was to be the first of hundreds of emails to our friends and family.

*　*　*

01.13 Thursday 3 May 2012
Hello to you all,

I am heartbroken to tell you that Cayle was involved in an IED explosion a few hours ago in Afghanistan. I do not have much news yet apart from the fact that both of his legs have now been amputated. He will be flown back to the UK within the next 24 hours. Seth has now arrived here from camp and is with me. We will head up to Birmingham together to the Queen Elizabeth Hospital tomorrow which is where Cayle will be taken. Your prayers are greatly appreciated during this difficult time.

Thank you,
Bronwyn

*　*　*

I now knew that Cayle was in the air being flown back to the UK. We would soon see the true scale of his horrific injuries. We didn't know then that we would watch for forty-eight long days as he fought for his life while in a coma. Nothing was ever going to be the same again. All I could do was picture Cayle, in a plane, in the darkness, flying home to us.

2. Bomb

Cayle
2 May 2012

We were in the Nahr-e Saraj North area of Afghanistan.

The day had started early with a 03:00 wake-up, a shave and a shower, and then on the flight line boarding the Chinook by 04:00. It was still dark when we landed in a poppy field in the green zone, the smell of rich earth and poppy flowers filling the cool air. As the Chinook lifted off and disappeared, the world seemed completely at peace. But there was work to be done and we set out on our task within moments of the helicopter's departure.

One of the primary roles of the Brigade Reconnaissance Force (BRF) was to find and destroy IED factories and secure high-priority targets. We had good intel that there was an IED factory in the area. We had heard a bit of chatter over the Icom radios. We could hear that there were Taliban in the area – the interpreter was telling us that they were around. We had searched multiple compounds through the day with no luck. Eventually in the late afternoon we made our way into a compound. In the compound itself we didn't really find any bomb-making materials. However, there was a smaller house just outside the compound – a sort of mud hut that had a shiny padlock on the door, an unusual item to find out there. The guys who were doing the searches found a huge amount of home-made explosives, pressure plates, detonators and other bomb-making equipment stored inside. The way we were trained to deal with it was to collect anything that may contain any forensic evidence … fingerprints, DNA and the like, or even building techniques that can be compared around the area to see if it's the same bomb makers who are making these devices. All the evidence was collected and then the explosives themselves were blown up, which levelled the compound they were stored in, raining down big chunks of wall into the next-door compound that we were all in. We were ducking for cover, hiding under anything we could. These massive pieces were raining down on us and we were all laughing and hooting in complete awe of how massive the explosion was. The shockwave of the blast shook the ground around us and lifted an enormous column of dust and debris high into the air.

Immediately the Taliban started chattering on the radio saying that they were going to 'hit' us, unaware that we could hear them. They were saying that they were going to ambush us, so we took a different route out of the compound to try to stay out of their way. Captain Harry Amos, being troop leader, took us out to the north of the compound, hoping to avoid the Taliban. Second Troop moved out, with us in First Troop bringing up the rear. At this stage I was third last in the patrol of fifteen. Second Troop were halfway across an open poppy field when they were ambushed and pinned down by a heavy rate of enemy fire. They hit the deck and were trying to hide in a completely exposed poppy field. Bullets buzzed and zipped past, kicking up dust as they tore through the field. We tried putting down some covering fire from closer to the compound as we were in better cover and were hoping to allow the guys who were pinned to get up and pull back into an irrigation ditch that was off to our right-hand side. We managed to suppress the incoming fire enough for them to get up and leg it into the relative safety of the ditch, at which point they then put down covering fire for us and we peeled around the back of them. Now in pretty good cover and more or less out of sight, the firing kind of stopped. First Troop were now up front leading the patrol. Matty (Trooper Matty Appleby) was now point man and up front, next was Shorty (Sergeant James Short), then myself, followed by Jacko (Corporal Ian Jackson) the medic. We were moving down the irrigation ditch that was orientated in more or less the direction we wanted to head back towards our patrol base.

To our left was the poppy field from where the Taliban had shot at us, and to the right was a ploughed field. This should generally mean it's safe to walk in because you can see the furrows, you can see how it's ploughed and generally there shouldn't be IEDs in those areas, and if there were they should be relatively easy to spot. Eventually the irrigation ditch got more and more dense. It was deep, boggy, stinking sludge and there was dense vegetation growing over and around the ditch, and because we were carrying so much kit we couldn't make any decent forward progress. The decision was made to push out to the right into the ploughed field and to continue making our way towards the safety of our previously established patrol base in a compound about 500 metres away.

I remember crawling out and just getting to my feet to kind of step off when it went 'pop'… I had initiated an IED.

The bang of the impact was pretty substantial. It knocked the wind out of me. I remember going skywards, landing quite heavily on my head. I remember the heat of the blast being scalding hot and the random impact. Initially I was in complete shock, so the pain wasn't there, but within a couple of seconds it was excruciating.

I remember thinking 'That was close, I have been hurt but I'll be ok … I better try to crawl into cover.' Thinking that I was lying on my back, I was trying to dig my heels into the ground to push myself into cover, whereas in fact I had landed flat on my face and I certainly wouldn't be moving my legs even though it felt like it; they had both been amputated immediately.

My right leg was dangling by a sinew, and my left was gone. I felt like there was boiling oil being poured all over me. It was red hot. Everything was just on fire and then came this overwhelming pain. I remember hearing Shorty, who had come running over to me, grabbing me round the back and rolling me over and saying everything was going to be alright. He did an amazing job. What you're taught when it comes to IEDs is that where there's one, there's more. The whole idea is that they injure somebody and then, because of the injury, they entice other people to come to treat that guy. So there's a huge risk to the people who are coming in to treat the wounded individual either through more IEDs or a further ambush.

Normally what you would have to do is come to clear the area around the casualty, which takes time, and I'm fairly certain that Shorty could see that there wasn't a great deal of that, so with complete disregard for his own safety, he came running in. We all carry four tourniquets in our clothing: two in your sleeves and two in your trouser pockets. My trouser ones were gone, but he immediately got the shoulder ones out and started to apply those. The medic, Jacko, who was behind me and who was blown backwards by the blast into the irrigation ditch, got out and came in to treat me. I remember them talking to me and saying, again, everything was going to be alright. Apparently I was making jokes with the guys and even said to Harry Amos, 'It looks like I won't be skiing this year', and, 'My tap dancing days are over, Boss.'

I remember Kirky (Lance Corporal Leon Kirkpatrick) and Matty helping out and making sure that I was packaged and as stable as possible, ready to be moved. Shorty then moved off to go and have a chat with Harry, who was already orchestrating the casualty evacuation (casevac) with the Medical Emergency Response Team (MERT) to fly me back to Camp Bastion. Harry and Shorty were so calm and professional throughout … really, really on the ball. The two of them had a face to face and immediately set about my extraction. Shorty had a look at his map, spoke to Harry and told him where he was going to set up the helicopter landing site. He then pushed out into a field just next to the ploughed field. Obviously, having seen that there were IEDs in the area, it needed to be cleared and they needed to set up a box of cleared space so that the helicopter could land without risk. So just after these guys have watched me being blown up, they've now got to walk foot over foot with a metal detector trying to find pressure plates and IEDs that quite often at that point didn't even have metal content any more – they were completely metal-free so the detectors wouldn't pick them up. Again, Shorty was commanding it. He detailed Ben (Trooper Ben Burdett) and Stoney, the military policeman with us, and they managed to get the whole box cleared. These men received no awards for bravery for what they did for me, but I promise you that this took courage beyond measure and I will be forever grateful.

At this point I had been given morphine and stabilised, put on a stretcher ready for the helicopter. It didn't take long before the helicopter came in. As it was coming in, a smoke grenade was popped to identify the position. The colour of smoke is agreed in advance so that the helicopter pilot knows it's the right landing point, otherwise the Taliban, who have access to all these sorts of things, could pop any colour of smoke and entice the helicopter in. I believe it was blue smoke that was popped, at which point the helicopter came and landed in the box that had been cleared. The guys ran me to the back of the Chinook over the uneven ground and did the handover with the medical team. I remember all of this in flashes. I remember the blast of heat from the engines of the Chinook as they ran me to the back of it and did the exchange with the team. They put me on the back of the Chinook and I was under the care of the doctor and med team, who then sedated me with a pretty good dose of ketamine, at which point I started to completely flake out. I don't really remember a great deal after that. The world began to go dark, but I could hear the whine of the engines and the distinctive thud of the propellers as we lifted off. They flew me to Role 3 in Camp Bastion where I was stabilised overnight and then flown to QEHB. I have very vague flashes of being in an aircraft and hearing the noise of an aircraft on flying back to the UK and then nothing particularly clear at all.

3. Boy

Bronwyn
19 February 1994

The fires always came in February, around Cayle's birthday. The bush was tinder dry and the strong south-easterly winds would whip in off the Atlantic Ocean and fan the smallest spark into a hurricane of flame. This year, the fire nearly swallowed us all.

Cayle was turning 8 that day. We were living in South Africa, in an old farmhouse on the Cape Peninsula. It was only an hour or so south of Cape Town, but our life was a world away from the big city. The boys would leave the house barefoot in the morning and vanish into the wilderness of forest and fynbos that stretched out from the 70-hectare farm in every direction. When I needed them, I'd call them home by blowing on a metal whistle and they'd emerge from the tree line, their little bodies stained red by the water and mud in the nearby clay dam.

Beyond the farm, everything was changing. Apartheid had been abolished in 1991, the African National Congress would soon win the April 1994 General Election, and Nelson Mandela was about to become the country's first black president. A new, better country was being born. But on the farm, we also occupied our own private world, where the laws and cycles of nature governed our lives. We never had much money, but Cayle, Seth, Richard and I found a kind of happiness in the wild.

Cayle had friends staying over the night the fire came. Richard and I were sleeping in the house while Cayle and Seth were camping outside with their friends in the back of our pick-up truck. In those days, as now, they'd sleep under the stars whenever possible.

Bang Bang Bang.

I woke up with a start and looked at the clock. 4.30 am.

Bang Bang Bang.

I clambered out of bed and went to the side door. It was our neighbour, Anton, and I could see the alarm in his eyes. Behind him, the sky was glowing orange, like an early dawn.

'There's a fire, Bronwyn. And it's coming this way.'

Richard appeared beside me.

'We've got to get the kids out of here. I'll take them down to the Pratts' place.'

'Muff' Pratt was the mother of one of Cayle's friends. She lived at the bottom of the mountain and as far as we could tell, her home would be missed by the blaze. It was the first safe place we could think of.

The boys were still in the back of the truck. Richard shouted,

'Stay where you are, boys, and keep your heads down – we're going ... now!'

Jumping into the driver's seat of the truck, he took off down the track with the reddening sky overhead. He was gone for around fifteen minutes, and all the while the fire continued its march towards us. By the time he got back, the blaze had reached the farm and a little after that, I watched as the flames closed like a curtain across the drive. We were trapped.

'Do you want anything out of the house, Bronwyn?'

'Like what?' I shouted.

'Photographs? Your passport?'

'What's the use? We're going to die in this thing.'

We ran down the drive and tried to beat out the flames – but it was hopeless. I could feel the searing heat on my face, the smoke scratching at my eyes and burning my lungs, and the first flames were soon licking the walls of the farmhouse.

'I'm going to burn to death!' I thought. 'Will I ever see my boys again?' I closed my eyes, fell to my knees on the dirt on the driveway, and prayed.

* * *

There was something so special about Cayle's arrival eight years earlier. He was born at 8.45 am on 19 February 1986 – 8lbs 15oz – and immediately became my whole world. The evening we brought Cayle home, I wrote an entry in his baby book:

> We brought you home from the hospital and ten minutes later, you started to scream. Daddy and I weren't quite sure what was wrong, so we decided to change your nappy. Well, no wonder you were complaining – as fast as we cleaned you, so it came out. You then proceeded to wee all over Daddy and all over the floor. Daddy and I couldn't stop laughing and you couldn't stop screaming ... my heart already ached with love.

I loved being a mother and cherished the fact that this beautiful little boy was mine. Perhaps it's selfish to say, but I knew that he'd love me unconditionally – at least until he was old enough to answer back. I still remember vividly his first laugh. He was 7 months old and he laughed when a cabbage was rolled across the kitchen floor. He seemed so startled when the noise came out of him – it was as if a car had backfired.

We were living in Durban on South Africa's Indian Ocean coast. Richard and I had both been born there and our families were close by. Cayle seemed to thrive in the outdoors and temperate climate from the very beginning. When we took him to the beach, he'd eat handfuls of sand and giggle when Richard held him in the waves.

'There's such a big world out there, Cayle,' I'd tell him, 'it's as big as you want it to be.'

He certainly loved to explore. He took his first steps aged 9 months and went everywhere barefoot and smiling, as if every corner of the house contained some unimaginable wonder, some gleaming, hidden treasure. But he rarely slept – at least he didn't sleep when I wanted to sleep. Perhaps he didn't have time for it. Every morning in the early hours I'd hear him moving about, so I'd go in to check – and there he'd be, sitting up in his cot, happily playing with his soft toys, perhaps even planning his escape.

It was the same with breastfeeding. I fed him until he was 13 months old – and then he just walked away. He didn't want to be tied to me and my boob; he wanted a cup. He wanted a cup so he could wander off and have whatever adventures 1-year-olds have. He craved independence, movement, experience.

'Fisssh.'

Cayle had said his first word at about 10 months old. There's a photo of him the day he was christened. A friend had given him a little wind-up fish as a gift, and he's sitting in a paddling pool with it, besotted. He loved that toy and learned the name of it before he said his first 'Mama' or 'Dada'.

Richard loved going fishing and Cayle soon followed suit. He later told me that his first memory was of fishing. He was 3 or 4 at the time and had gone to the beach with Richard and Richard's friend, Derek. Cayle was hit by a wave and recalls Derek reaching down and yanking him out of the water, spluttering and blinded by the brine.

Three years after Cayle, Seth was born in 1989. Shortly after that, Richard started his own business as an aluminium shower door and balustrade manufacturer, and I bought a take-away business in an industrial area. The menu included a variety of curries, one of the most popular being 'Walkie talkie', which was made using chicken feet and beaks, much to the boys' amusement and something they still speak about to this day. However, with us each running our own business, it meant working long hours, which took its toll on our boys, who were both in day-care. In 1993 we decided to make a new start by moving to Cape Town, specifically the very rural Cape Peninsula. Richard and I thought a wilder kind of childhood would give the boys a good grounding.

Sharing the 70 hectares with six other dwellings, we rented the main farmhouse, a magnificent 100-year-old stone building with beautiful wooden floors. We would usually access the house via one of two doors into the kitchen – one leading from the driveway and through the beautifully aromatic herb garden, the other, more frequently used, facing in the direction of the rest of the farm dwellings. The kitchen led into a small walk-through study area and on to a spacious and very airy lounge with a huge stone fireplace. Off the lounge, a long passageway led to three enormous bedrooms and a ridiculously massive family bathroom with a bathtub to match.

The twentieth century had, however, left the farm far behind. It was without municipal running water or mains power. Our lighting came from candles or paraffin lamps and we cooked on gas. The boys couldn't just turn on a television or open a computer; they had to entertain themselves in the wilderness. Instead of cartoons, they had a rope swing; instead of computer games, they'd battle imaginary zombies; instead of plastic toys, they'd build go-karts and career down the hillside, bloodying their elbows and knees. And there were always snakes, scorpions or spiders to find, then run away from.

Our drinking water came from a freshwater spring on the farm. All of our other water was pumped up from the muddy clay dam behind the piggery into a huge 200-litre drum on the roof of the house. It was heated using a donkey boiler system, Cayle usually being the one to chop the wood for the fire underneath it. He's still got a chipped tooth after accidentally hitting himself in the face with the axe.

There would only ever be enough hot water for one bath and we'd all take our turn in sharing it. The water was dark brown, like Coca-Cola, and all you could see was the boys' heads poking out of the steaming, stained water. The bath was one of our simple luxuries.

We ate a lot of lentils. There's broke and then there's broke broke, and we were the latter at that point. We used to joke about 'lentils and stones' being on the menu. The lentils were unrefined and gritty and you'd have to crunch your way through them. Some days we'd have a few potatoes too and, to make things a little more exciting for the boys, I'd occasionally add a drop of blue, red or green food colouring to mashed potatoes and they loved it. There was the odd day when we didn't even have lentils, but a neighbour would usually give us some vegetables from her garden. When there's nothing to eat but cabbage soup, it's amazing how quickly children stop being fussy eaters.

But they did still get the odd treat. When they were a bit older, the boys discovered that a tractor transported trailer-loads of out-of-date or misshapen cakes from a nearby bakery to the local pig farm. They'd jump into the trailer and unload as much as they could carry – cup cakes, Swiss rolls, sticky buns, biscuits – and then run into the woods to gorge themselves. Occasionally, the haul was a little mouldy, but for the boys, these cakes were the spoils of war.

It was a world apart from the suburbia that was only a few kilometres away at the bottom of the mountain. During the week I would twice daily make the trip down the pass to drop Cayle at school. When Cayle's friends came to play after school, their mothers would sometimes arrive in tears having driven up to collect them. The access up steep, winding Red Hill Road, which led to the farm, was too overwhelming for some. The children sometimes found it scary, too. I still remember trying to get hold of the parents of one boy who had come to play. He was terrified by the forest and the open space. He'd never seen a wild mushroom before, and when he did, it was the final straw. He was in floods of tears, begging to go home. What we'd become accustomed to as normal life was definitely not normal for most people.

When it came to paying for school fees, we did not have the money. I approached the school office about our finances and it was agreed that in lieu of paying cash, I would paint the exterior of the multi-storey school building. What I didn't share with them was my extreme fear of heights, but I knew then that it was my only option. Donned in a pair of bright pink and yellow dungarees and a large sun hat to protect my fair skin, I became a familiar sight clinging to the top of an extension ladder with a paintbrush in one hand and container of paint in the other. It took me many weeks to work my way around the entire school, but I paid our dues and secured Cayle's place at the school for the year.

Winters on the farm were harsh. The old house was never properly sealed. We'd light a fire in the lounge and you wouldn't feel the faintest flicker of heat unless you were sitting directly in front of it. All the warmth went straight up the chimney or out through the yawning gaps in the windows, doors and floorboards. On very cold nights I'd fill empty plastic bottles with warm water and put them into the boys' beds. You get used to the bitter cold, though, just as you learn to love lentils.

Normally barefoot, Cayle would wear a pair of blue and yellow rubber wellington boots in winter. They got pretty hot and stinky, so Richard's eventual solution was to take a hot copper pipe and burn holes in the top of them. The result was most likely the world's first pair of Crocs. He got teased over the boots, but he just got on with it. Cayle understood we had very little money and soon realised that experiences, rather than things, would bring him happiness.

Cayle became very protective of Seth. One day they were out playing in the pine forest when they stumbled upon an old naval dumping ground. Seth, 4 years old at the time, stood on a smashed port bottle that sliced right through his foot. Cayle, who himself was only 7, carried him all the way to the farmhouse on his back without a whimper. We loaded the boys into the truck and raced Seth off to the doctor's room where he needed eight or nine stitches. While I crouched on the floor as I thought I was going to pass out during the procedure, Cayle watched intrigued, unflinching.

It was clear from an early age that Cayle wanted adventures further afield too. Even when he was very young, he loved the idea of mountaineering. He'd read about the exploits of Sean Wisedale, the first South African to climb the highest mountain on each of the seven continents, and talked about following in his footsteps. His uncle Keith had been a forward observer in the artillery, plus he had travelled extensively. Keith would tell tall tales of his exploits and Cayle would listen intently, absorbing all the information he could.

Being short of money certainly didn't stop us doing things. Most weekends we would be busy – either camping, out walking, or the boys would be fishing or exploring. Richard made sure to keep them occupied and 'off the streets and out of trouble'. We still had family living in Durban and we'd make long road trips to visit them, the boys riding in the back of our 'bakkie' – a Mazda B-Series pick-up. We couldn't afford a canopy to cover the back, so Richard rigged up a system using bright blue plastic sheeting stretched over bent aluminium bars. We'd put a mattress in the back and Cayle and Seth travelled for hundreds of miles that way, reading Asterix comics in the weird yellow-green light, or leaning out the back, the breeze blowing on their cheeks.

South Africa is a beautiful, diverse country. You can be in a baking hot desert, then drive for a couple of hours over a mountain pass to the coast and find yourself in a lush, verdant forest. The mountains of the Cederberg are bone-dry in summer, and the rains come in winter; the Drakensberg mountains in summertime are emerald green, and they in turn go crisp and brown in winter. One night, up high by the Golden Gate on the border of Lesotho, it was too cold to camp, so we had to splash out to stay in a bed and breakfast. Taking every opportunity he could to educate the boys, Richard poured his mug of water over the roof of the car and it instantly froze solid. The boys were entranced.

Sometimes we combined Richard's business trips with leisure and we'd go further afield. We'd get permission to take the boys out of school and we explored Namibia extensively: Walvis Bay, Swakopmund, sand-boarding on Dune 7, the highest dune in Namibia. Experiencing real life was better than being in a classroom. We were camping in the wilderness one full-moon night when before our eyes a cactus opened up into bloom; big white flowers bursting in the desert.

On another night, we were preparing the meat for the 'braai' (barbecue) when Cayle noticed the glinting eyes of a black-backed jackal, its face appearing out of the gloom. It grabbed a plastic plate in its mouth and ran off. All we could hear then was the 'clack, clack, clack' as it tried to hold it between its teeth. The boys later found the plate covered in drool and with one side chewed. From then on that yellow plate was known as the Jackal Plate. It always brought back vivid memories when dinner was served on it.

And so life went on, simple but happy, with two little boys growing up into adventurers.

* * *

I will never be completely sure how the fire truck made it to the house, but there it was and all around us were men, battling back the flames. They were mostly men from a nearby township, wearing everyday clothes with wet rags over their faces to protect them from the smoke. Their bravery saved our lives.

While the fire had licked the walls, the main house was still intact. The fire moved swiftly to destroy some of the outbuildings, and the sound of gas bottles exploding in the intense heat could be heard across the farm and, I'm sure, beyond. Once the smaller blazes in the yard had been extinguished, the main fire moved on, destroying the forest in its path.

That bushfire raged in the area for days. We, and our home, had survived, but when we brought the boys back, most of what they had known had gone: the pine forest, the tree swing, all turned to ash. Our wilderness was a smouldering, smoking mess and Cayle, walking in his gum boots over the hot, grey earth, would keep finding the charred remains of the animals we had shared it with: chickens and ducklings, even tortoises and snakes.

He was only 8, and small for his age, but there was a growing maturity to him that made me proud. It was sometimes hard to see in the fresh features of my beautiful little boy, but Cayle was becoming a young man.

4. Mother

Bronwyn

Exactly one month to the day after the fire, my father very unexpectedly passed away in Durban. I had had a strong bond with him and the year we had been apart while I was living with my own family near Cape Town had been very hard for me. We spoke regularly on the phone but it wasn't the same as being in his company. His input in my life had been invaluable and he had always been available for me when I needed advice. Now I had to come to terms with the fact that I would never see him again.

I was born in Durban, South Africa in 1960, the second eldest of five children – four girls and one boy. Of course we had our quarrels when we were growing up, but to this day we have never had a major fallout, which I believe is unusual and even envied by many families. We are constantly in contact with each other and my mother used to say that her wealth was in her children. I believe this to be true – for her and for me.

Apartheid was very much alive in South Africa in my younger years. I vividly remember asking my parents on one of our beach excursions why the beaches had signs with 'Whites Only' written on them. And why the public toilets had two sections – 'Whites' and 'Non Whites'. It never made any sense to me. Then there was the law regarding 'dompas', which directly translated from Afrikaans means 'dumb pass'. All black people outside the confines of their government-designated areas were legally required to carry passbooks. Police officers could apprehend any black person and ask to see it. Failure to produce the dompas resulted in being arrested and imprisoned if one could not pay the required fine. Curfews were imposed and by 10 pm every night, black people had to be off the streets. It doesn't take much to bring back a flood of memories of standing at my bedroom window, looking out onto our little street watching police officers patrolling in our tiny suburb, ensuring that no 'offenders' were out beyond time. Many of the officers carried sjamboks, a long stiff whip originally made of rhinoceros hide. These Pass laws were one of the dominant features of South Africa's Apartheid system until it was finally abolished in 1991 – not a moment too soon.

Dad had held the position of General Manager of the South African Sugar Association for more than twenty-five years, a busy career involving a lot of international travel. Mom was a home executive, a full-time job but without the corresponding pay, and when she wasn't taxiing one of us to or from school or some or other extracurricular activity, she busied herself with flower arranging, working with aromatherapy oils, and writing the occasional article for a magazine. There were also numerous business dinners to be planned and catered for.

My father was the sole beneficiary of an English aunt's estate, and my parents used the inheritance to build a large five-bedroomed house with a swimming pool in a beautiful suburb on the outskirts of Durban. Needing assistance at home, they employed help in the form of Ethel the live-in maid, and Timothy the gardener. Meal-times had to be a fairly regimented affair. Ethel would prepare the menu Mom had planned, and us children would eat at the table in the breakfast room, which was tucked to one side of the kitchen. The posh dining room next door was reserved for my parents' quiet meals when Dad was home, and their business dinner parties; very seldom were we invited to eat in there unless it was a special occasion. We had a separate lounge from their formal one, but ours was much more comfortable and fun to be in. Sunday evenings were my favourite time of the week. My father would hire a reel-to-reel film and we would invite the neighbours and extended family over. We'd get to choose a few bags of sweets to be shared among us, divided into bowls that were constantly passed around. We children lay spread out on our backs on the floor, gazing up at the flickering images on the wall while the massive projector whirred loudly in the background. Whenever Dad went away on a business trip, I was given the task of projectionist, a position I took very seriously.

My relationship with my mom was a little more complex. Mom was the youngest of four children, but her father had deserted them when she was very young, so she never knew him. There was a large age gap between the older children and the younger two, and the older moved out of home as soon as they were able, leaving my grandmother struggling financially to support my mom and her brother Mike. When Nana had an income things were fine, but often she had to send Mom and Mike off to distant relatives or place them in an orphanage for long periods. When I was maybe 7 or 8 years old, I thought Mom didn't really like me because she never showed me any affection. I used to look on with envy at other children with their mothers and just long for a hug. I vowed that one day if ever I had children of my own, I would shower them with love and hugs and so much affection; I'd constantly tell them how much I loved them.

Then in my mid-teens, Mom started to open up a little about her own upbringing, including the beatings that took place in the orphanage, and the lack of physical contact with her own mother. She spoke of the anger that seemed to consume Nana and how hard it had been to have a mother/daughter relationship with her. With this insight, I began to see my mom through different eyes and things improved between us.

I was a very timid child, scared of my own shadow. I tried not to do anything that would upset anyone because the thought of getting into trouble terrified me. I never bunked a day off school, and to this day I have never put a cigarette to my lips or tried any recreational drugs. I always wanted to be liked and became a people-pleaser for fear of rejection. Being very shy and softly spoken, I didn't have many friends at school, but I connected with a handful of girls. When I was 15, one of them introduced me to her church, which was far more charismatic than what I had been used to in my Sunday School years. Seeds were sown over the following eighteen months.

I finished my schooling in 1977 and the following year I qualified as a Legal Secretary, going on to work in a bank for five years. It had been a lifelong ambition of mine to try to make sure everyone liked me and I shied away from confrontational situations whenever possible. Unfortunately this hindered me from climbing the corporate ladder.

Richard and I married in 1983. My parents divorced that same year and, after a bumpy few months when I continued to see my dad, which upset Mom, my relationship with her strengthened. I'd hug her whenever we met up and slowly she got used to the affection.

Things changed for me when I became a mother and I felt I had a purpose. After years of floundering I suddenly felt anchored by my role as mom to my two very special kids and I felt confident that I was doing a good job raising them. I focused everything on my boys. I have lived my life through them and I wanted to encourage them to be themselves, not influenced by what others thought of them. Fear had paralysed me my whole life and I prayed it would not be the same for them.

Although always in the back of my mind, Christianity was not a huge part of my life. Moving from Durban to the farm in the Cape in 1994 was a fresh start for us and in the harshness of our new environment, Christianity became very important to me. We joined a local church and I was able to connect with like-minded people. Finally I felt that I belonged somewhere and I began to make new friends, some of whom I still have in my life today and whose friendships I truly value.

During the first sixteen years of our marriage, Richard opened a number of businesses and although I always worked with him, my heart was never fully committed to any of them. I'd been creative my whole life, whether it be sketching for hours as a young child, making my boys clothes when they were young, learning new craft skills, baking cakes, and even trying my hand at screen printing. I knew something was missing and it wasn't until 1999 that I finally found my passion. A friend invited me to join her at a watercolour painting class and I was instantly hooked. I'd not attempted this type of art before but I loved it. I loved being able to create and express myself. Encouraged by my tutor, four years later I opened my own art school and began teaching adults in the mornings and children in the afternoons. My confidence grew as my students enjoyed my lessons as much as I did. My classes were full and my register had thirty-seven student names in it.

Then, early in 2006, my life shifted. Cayle told us that he was serious about moving to the UK to join the British Army. Even after the abolishment of Apartheid, the state of affairs in South Africa was not hopeful. Seth, too, was keen to complete his schooling in a country that he hoped would offer him more opportunities. With that in mind, both boys began making enquiries about emigrating.

My mom had recently been diagnosed with terminal breast cancer and I was trying to spend as much time with her as possible when I wasn't teaching art or helping Richard with our business. In April, the boys' applications for Ancestral Visas to move to the UK were approved and I began the preparations for their departures, including booking flights and securing accommodation for them in Dartmouth. We waved farewell to Seth when he flew out from Cape Town on 20 May. Ten days later I was at Mom's bedside when she lost her battle with cancer. My sisters were there too and we held her hands as she drew her last breath. I couldn't bear the thought that she was alone, so I climbed into the bed next to her and held her while we waited for the doctor to arrive to certify her death.

Two weeks later, Cayle left for the UK. Three important people had disappeared from my life within the space of a month and it suddenly felt very empty. My family and friends and my art classes kept me going, but I was lost without my boys and my mom, and I was prone to bursting into tears regularly. I'd totally lived my life for and through my children and I was suffering seriously with empty nest syndrome.

A year later, we assessed our lives and Richard and I made the decision to rent out our Cape Town house and join our sons in the UK. We sold the business, I closed my art school and with one suitcase each, we boarded a plane to a whole new world. I'd been to the UK a few times on holiday, but for Richard it was the first time and a complete culture shock.

We too moved to Dartmouth and I was fortunate enough to be offered full-time employment seven months after arriving in the UK. I held the position of manager, working for a local artist running his second shop, for close to nine years before being made redundant. I am grateful for the opportunity it gave me to remain in the UK to gain my British Citizenship.

I settled well into life in the UK because I was near the boys and I was also able to take annual trips back to South Africa to see my family. Richard struggled to find work in his preferred marine engineering field as he didn't have the appropriate paperwork for the UK. This put a lot of pressure on us and our marriage broke down. Richard and I separated early in 2010 and divorced eighteen months later, but we remain friends. I have never regretted emigrating, despite missing my siblings terribly. I dread to even think about how hard it would have been to cope with Cayle's incident if I still lived in South Africa.

From the outside my life looks to be full of achievement, but if I have a regret, it is that my lack of confidence hindered me from doing much more. I was determined, as a result, that I would encourage my boys to get out and make the most of their lives.

5. Man

Bronwyn

In November 2003, aged 16, Cayle completed his schooling and within months (and with a lot of encouragement from Richard) he became a river guide working in Namibia. Before my eyes, I watched my son transform as he thrived in the outdoors, soon realising all his strengths and leadership capabilities. The immense open spaces, huge star-sprinkled night skies, and the excitement of occasional wild waters cutting through the red and black-baked mountains of Namibia fuelled Cayle's hunger to want more from life.

Six months later, a two-year work/holiday visa in his South African passport offered him the opportunity to broaden his horizons and he headed for the UK. However, feeling the energy being sapped out of him daily, his lungs filled with smog, a few days in the hustle and bustle of central London was more than enough. With the allure of what he hoped would be more like the surroundings to which he was accustomed, he applied for a job as a barman at a golf club on the outskirts of Dartmouth in Devon. The clean air and wider vistas of the UK's South West coast would be far more suitable for him.

Ten months after landing in the country and having worked very long hours, Cayle had saved enough money to go travelling in Europe. We decided that I should join him and eventually we settled on a trip to Greece and Italy. I flew out from South Africa and, after spending a few days with him in Dartmouth meeting his new friends, we headed up to Heathrow Airport and flew out to Athens.

We had one or two moments during those first few days together when I tried to take charge, but a year of living abroad had turned him into an extremely capable young man. I no longer needed to make decisions for him and it was a little alien to me at first. We caught a ferry from Athens down to Santorini and then island-hopped our way back up to the mainland. When we could, we hired a scooter to do some sightseeing and basically laughed our way around each island.

For six weeks we camped and backpacked our way around Greece and then Italy. We tasted a variety of foods, drank whatever the locals drank, explored extensively wherever we went, but most of all we bonded. We spent hours lying beside our tent, under the stars, chatting about anything and everything. The trip was exactly what we both needed and we had a lot of time to catch up and ponder the future. I think we realised that the memories from that trip would be cemented in our hearts forever.

Our time in Europe confirmed for Cayle that he was ready to head home to South Africa and we boarded a plane back to Cape Town. Within weeks he was training hard in anticipation of climbing Mount Kilimanjaro, which he summited on 25 October 2005, fulfilling a lifelong dream. But something was niggling at him and he was restless.

Over the years, Cayle had spoken relentlessly about joining the British Army. His paternal grandfather had been in the military, and his father and uncles had been conscripted into the South African Army. Their frequent telling of animated tales had only encouraged him more. He had made some enquiries about the British Army while in the UK and he let us know that he was serious about joining. With Cayle having spent time in Dartmouth back in 2004/2005, he had made contacts in the area and it seemed a sensible place for the boys to move to.

On 22 October 2006, Cayle enlisted with the Parachute Regiment based in Catterick, North Yorkshire – about as far away from Dartmouth as could be. The prospect of him finally joining the military had him training long hours and running an average of twenty miles a day. With a regimented gym session thrown in either morning or noon, it soon became a reality. Although he thought the training would stand him in good stead, Cayle suffered badly with stress fractures in his legs, which he had developed through overtraining on the hills around Dartmouth.

A few months into the rigorous Parachute Regiment basic training, the fractures worsened and he was admitted to the rehabilitation centre.

It was there where he met Gerhard Roos. Also a South African but from an Afrikaans-speaking family, his accent was still thick and easily recognisable. Both of them weighed the same, had the same boot size, were the same height, and were in rehab for the same injury. They soon became friends. Both were medically discharged from the Parachute Regiment in October 2007, after which they went on a trip around Europe, ending up in Corsica where they lived like wild men in the bush on a peninsula for a month. This trip cemented their friendship.

Once back in Dartmouth, Cayle befriended a gentleman by the name of Chris Dick. Chris needed some gardening and boat maintenance work done and Cayle accepted the job. An intelligent, well-spoken and highly respected man, Chris had been a brigadier in the Royal Tank Regiment and had done a stint as second in command with the then 13th/18th Hussars, who later amalgamated with the 15th/19th Hussars to become the Light Dragoons in 2001. Nothing ever seemed too much trouble for him and the two of them would while away the hours chatting about all things military. With Chris's encouragement, Cayle eventually opted to apply for the Light Dragoons.

By July 2007, Richard and I had emigrated to the UK. In May 2008, Gerhard, now fondly known to us as Roos or Roosie, came to live with us while he and Cayle began their endeavours to rejoin the military. Both of them were accepted into the Light Dragoons.

Both completed the basic training, and at the passing-out parade in October 2009 we were proudly surprised when Cayle received a number of awards.

Following an incredible trip to Jordan, thanks to an invitation from King Abdullah of Jordan (who is the Regimental Colonel in Chief), Cayle was transferred across to 'B' Squadron as he had been selected for the Brigade Reconnaissance Force (BRF) and training for his role as a sharpshooter was to begin. BRF training included travelling to Kenya and Canada to participate in large-scale exercises in different terrains.

Fast-forward to December 2011 and finally Cayle was able to fulfil his life-long desire to try skiing. He was invited by Captain Harry Amos to join a group heading out to Verbier in Switzerland for six weeks. A large number of regiments would be going out, including other Armoured Corp regiments. It was expected that each unit would include a few complete novices as well as more experienced skiers. The intention of the exercise was to get the guys up to a standard to compete in various races. The races were to establish placings and from there those who qualified would move on to further racing in France. Cayle did very well and the Light Dragoons won every team event, but unfortunately did not move on to France as they needed to get back to the UK for more BRF training before deployment.

While out there, Cayle met Alex, the owner of a paramotor training school. Over a few drinks, Alex, Harry and Cayle started discussing flying and when Alex mentioned that he wanted to teach wounded soldiers how to fly, Cayle said he was keen to learn and he even joked darkly that he was off to Afghanistan in a few months so 'I may just be eligible to apply'.

Cayle's training for his role with the BRF had been extensive and with a final assessment on Salisbury Plain in early March, the BRF had established itself as competent and ready to deploy to Afghanistan on Operation Herrick 16 at the end of March 2012.

6. Farewell

Bronwyn
March 2012

Richard Baker had been a massive part of our lives since the boys emigrated from South Africa to the UK in 2006. He owned a house in Dartmouth and although he worked away in London and travelled extensively for business, he and his wife had opened up a cocktail bar in town and both of my boys had worked on and off for them. Despite the age difference, the three of them were extremely close; so close in fact that Rich called me 'Mom'.

The weekend before deploying to Afghanistan, Cayle and Roos were in Dartmouth to say farewell to family and friends. They were due to leave town the following morning and up at Rich's house that Sunday afternoon we took a few fun photographs, the last photos taken with the boys before they flew out. As we were leaving the house, Cayle had pulled Rich aside,

'You've got my Mom, right? Your word? You've got my Mom?'

With Cayle's departure now imminent, I lay awake that night considering what the worst-case scenario might be regarding his deployment to a country with such a high incident rate. Would he cope under the extreme pressure of coming under attack? Would he crack or hold steady? I dreaded even thinking about it, but what if he was injured – how would he come to terms with it? And how would I? I knew that he was highly trained and had excelled in every course he had undertaken; he could not have been more prepared for the task that lay before him. I thought back over Cayle's life and realised that, for a young man of 26, he had made the most of every single opportunity that had presented itself to him. Then I closed my eyes and prayed for protection over him.

I was up early the next morning to cook him a full English breakfast. We sat at my kitchen table chatting.

'I could not be prouder of you, Cayle. I never would have chosen for you to join the military but that's for selfish reasons. I will always support you because I know that you love it.'

'I do, Ma. I feel so ready for this.'

I had savoured the precious pockets of time we'd spent together over the past ten days while he had been on leave, but now I had to let him go. He hauled his backpack on and we headed down the narrow stairs and out into the bright sunlight. Standing in the square outside my flat with the St Saviour's Church bells chiming ten o'clock, we hugged and said our farewells. My heart was pounding as I clung to him, reluctant to let go but knowing that he was excited to get going. He climbed into his car to drive away and, letting down his window, his last words to me were:

'Agh, I'll be okay, Ma. Love you.'

I leaned in for a final hug.

'I love you too my precious child. Take care.'

Gulping while blinking to hold back the tears, I put a brave smile on my face and waved enthusiastically until his car had turned the corner of Anzac Street and was out of sight. Then I leaned my shoulder heavily against the shop door frame and I began to sob. My heart literally ached with the love I felt for my son.

7. Body

Bronwyn
3 May 2012

I had received the news of Cayle's incident less than twelve hours ago. Sleep evaded me, so I was up early to shower and dress. It was spring, but nevertheless I put Cayle's body warmer over my shirt and went into his bedroom. I sat on the edge of his bed and I could hear the street beginning to bustle with the early risers. How could life be going on as normal out there while I was reeling from the devastating news we had been given? Dropping my head, I began to weep softly as I prayed for my son's life to be spared.

At what I deemed the more reasonable hour of 8 am, I phoned my employers to inform them that I would need to be away for a few days. I also rang my friend Betty, who rushed down to see me, reprimanding me for not having contacted her the night before.

When she arrived, I was sitting on my sofa with my face buried deep in my hands, sobbing, 'My beautiful boy, my beautiful boy.'

Wanting to be as helpful as she could, she offered to pack a bag for me.

'How long will you be gone for, love?' she enquired.

'If you could pack enough clothes for three days that should be enough, thanks Betty,' I said.

Warrant Officer Armstrong arrived at midday to collect Seth and me to drive us up to Birmingham. It is military policy that immediate family do not drive themselves after receiving such news because of the emotional stress they are under. It flashed through my mind that Seth should not have driven himself home.

As the vehicle pulled away from Dartmouth, I handed my phone to Seth, who took control of contacting those we felt needed to be informed. I sat in the back trying desperately to compose myself, wanting to be of some assistance to him. I could not stop the image of Cayle from racing through my mind, the problem being that I now had no real visual reference to go by.

* * *

The first person Seth had phoned after receiving the news was Rich Baker. He was in Ireland on business and his wife organised an early morning flight out for him back to the UK. The driver of the taxi to Dublin airport waived his fee, and when the adrenaline that raced through his body caused Rich to vomit into the gutter as he climbed out of the vehicle, the driver leapt out and gave him a can of Coke and offered to escort him inside. Unfortunately the airline didn't show the same compassion; when he explained the situation and why he hadn't been able to print his boarding pass, he was told to find a computer and pay for it to be printed.

* * *

Four hours after leaving Dartmouth we pulled up outside the Welfare Offices on the outskirts of Birmingham. Already waiting for us was Rich, pacing up and down the car park. He opened the car door for me and all three of us embraced.

Ushered into a counselling room, we were informed by a Welfare Officer of the procedure we could expect over the following few hours. Relieved and amazed, we were told that, for as long as it would be necessary, we had free use of a fully equipped three-bedroom apartment a short distance from the hospital. An hour later and our heads overflowing with information, Rich drove us over to the apartment to drop our few belongings.

At 6 pm prompt, Warrant Officer Armstrong knocked on the apartment door, ready to transport us across town. We sped towards the newly opened QEHB and my first view of the three massive pods reminded me of a spaceship resting on a hill, a sight that was to become very familiar over the following few months.

Keen to escape the suffocating confines of the vehicle, we leapt from the car the moment it came to a standstill outside the main entrance. Pushing through the hospital doors, Seth, Rich and I took our first glimpse of the ground floor. A Costa coffee shop was on the right and a branch of WHSmith on the left. We had about fifteen minutes to spare before Cayle was likely to be transported in, so Rich bought me a hardback, lined notebook and a pen from WHSmith so I could start writing things down.

We asked at the reception desk where we would need to be – the next floor up. Access was via the lifts or a couple of flights of stairs; we opted for the stairs and climbed them two at a time, heading straight to the first-floor restaurant. Scanning the room, we determined where the best vantage point would be, settling on the casual seating area that had a clear view of the hospital entrance through the double-height floor-to-ceiling windows.

The sun was still high in the sky at 6.25 pm as we stood guard at the window. Blue flashing lights in the distance heralded the arrival of the speeding motorcade – two police cars and two police motorcycles escorting the ambulance carrying the precious cargo of my son's shattered body from Birmingham Airport to the rear of the hospital. The escort had reduced the travel time from forty minutes to seventeen, every single minute vital to his chances of survival. I was immensely relieved that the lights were still flashing as it suggested he must be alive. My entire body was covered in goosebumps, my throat tightened and my heart was pounding. It dawned on me that I would soon see my child and that the blurred image in my mind would be replaced by brutal reality. Emotions from nerves to fear, and anxiety to anticipation, raced through me in seconds as we watched the last of the motorcade disappearing behind the building.

Moving from our vantage point, we asked a passing nurse where we needed to wait. Ushered to a totally nondescript counselling room, the three of us sat huddled together on blue padded chairs for what seemed like an eternity while we waited for Cayle to be settled into the Intensive Trauma Unit (ITU). Rich was trying his best to encourage us with his positive words.

'Cayle will be fine. He's always been strong, physically fit, and most of all stubborn. He's not going to give up.'

A full hour after we had spotted the motorcade, the door to the counselling room slid open and a group of nine medical staff entered. Brief introductions revealed that four of them were from the team who had been aboard the C-17 (Aeromed) bringing Cayle back from Afghanistan.

Soldiers who are injured are issued a patient diary. Entries are made into the diary either by those working with the patient or by visitors.

<u>11:10 am, 3 May</u>

You are now on the flight back to RCDM Birmingham. We are the C-Cast escorting you home. You have two doctors, two nurses, medic and MDSS (Medical and Dental Servicing Section) technician on board to ensure your safe return to the UK. Our hopes and prayers are with you for a speedy recovery.

Exhausted from the non-stop flight, they remained standing as they gave a brief summary of Cayle's condition during the long flight.

The three of us sat in silence, numb from shock, trying desperately to absorb the enormity of the news just delivered, and despite their prompting, all questions evaded us.

Taking this as their cue to leave, one of them leaned towards me with an outstretched arm:

'I'm sure you want these.' Dangling from his fingers were Cayle's dog tags.

As I reached out to take them, the impact of my action slammed home. The identification details were proof that this was not a nightmare from which I would soon wake; this was reality. I clutched the tags tightly into my palm, silently thanking God that both tags were still on the chain, while nodding my appreciation to the deliverer. The tags jingled together as I slipped the chain over my head and tucked them inside Cayle's body warmer, close to my heart.

Responsibility was now handed over to the new team consisting of Group Captain (GC) Ian Sargeant (Consultant Trauma and Orthopaedics Surgeon), Lieutenant Colonel (LC) Al Mountain (Consultant Surgeon) and Wing Commander William Van Niekerk (Consultant Plastic and Aesthetic Cosmetic Surgeon). Also present were RAF Sergeant Laura Greaves, who was the Duty Critical Care Nurse (DCCN) that week, and Senior Sister Hazel Lane (or 'the nut' as she introduced herself to us), the DCCN responsible for Cayle that first night.

Sitting down, Ian Sargeant took control from the onset:

'What do you know about his injuries?'

Between the three of us we tried to recall what we could.

'Please would you go over them again for us?' Seth asked.

'I believe in being 100 per cent honest,' said Ian, 'and having briefly assessed him, I would say that, although his external injuries are severe, our biggest issue is going to be his lungs.'

Noticing our puzzled looks, he began explaining how the force of the explosion had crushed Cayle's lungs and that without a doubt this would be a massive problem within a few days when the bruising came out.

'It also seems that he was in or near water at the time,' he continued, 'and the diseases that are carried in filthy water could be something else to consider.'

He went on to say, 'The new body armour that Cayle was wearing includes something called a nappy and this has undoubtedly prevented any damage to his genital area. This will play a massive role further down the line when it comes to his mental recovery.'

William Van Niekerk went on, 'The damage to his face is extensive but at the moment we have bigger issues to consider. We will close the wounds around his mouth to stem the bleeding, but for now we need to concentrate on saving his life.'

'What you should be made aware of,' continued Ian, 'is that if Cayle had sustained these injuries in the UK, even a few miles away from this hospital, the chance of him surviving would be minimal. To get an ambulance and paramedics out to him would have taken too long – it was the instant action of the medic and the men around him at the time of the incident that have no doubt saved his life.'

The image of my son began to blur even more in my mind as I realised that he would not look like the young man who I had waved goodbye to a few weeks earlier. The picture being painted was one I was unable to envisage, one I had hoped never to have to see. I felt numb as I desperately tried to retain every word being spoken. My mind had wanted to block out what I was hearing but, even at such a time, I somehow comprehended that there were others waiting for any titbit of news and the three of us were their only chance of an update. Throughout my life I have had comments about how incredible my memory is; this would be the test. In some strange way, it helped me keep my composure and concentration.

We'd been bombarded with a volley of information and by the time the briefing was done it was 7.40 pm and Cayle was due to be in surgery twenty minutes later. Sister Hazel asked if we would like a few minutes with him. In the moments it took us to reach the ITU ward, she told us that we should prepare ourselves for the worst.

After a quick tutorial by Hazel on ITU ward entry etiquette, we meticulously rubbed our hands and arms with the compulsory sanitiser from the dispenser at the entrance to the ward. Following closely behind her, Rich, Seth and I gained access to a whole new world, me holding tightly to Seth's arm. I stared blindly at the back of Hazel's head as we walked in silence, not daring to look either side of me to where the beeps and buzzes of machines were coming from. I was mentally preparing myself for the moment of truth as my heart pounded and my mouth became dry. It struck me that there was no hospital smell, something that had always made me anxious.

We approached the bed-space and Hazel drew back the curtain. Cayle had been shrouded in a sheet up to just below his closed eyes. I gasped at the impact of seeing the sheet just drop away where his beautiful strong legs should have been. Tears spilled over and slid down my cheeks. In stark contrast to the physical state of his body, he looked so peaceful, a result of the heavily induced coma he was in.

It was shocking how short he seemed in the bed. Cayle had been a strapping young man at six feet tall, and to see that there was so little of him left knocked me sideways. I tried to blink the tears away. Hazel had taken his right hand out from under the cover so that we could hold it. Letting go of mine, Seth moved straight over to hold Cayle's lifeless hand in his. Rich pleaded with Hazel,

'Would it be possible for Mom to kiss Cayle's forehead? She needs to have some physical contact with him.'

Taking my hand, she and I weaved our way, ducking and dipping, through the tubes and wires to reach the head of the bed, which had been slightly raised. I tentatively stood up on my toes, bent down and kissed my precious son on the top of his head. A ventilation tube protruded from his mouth, slightly holding the sheet from his face. As I lifted my head to move away, I caught a glimpse. In that split second I could see that his top lip looked like thinly sliced raw meat with a gaping wound running in an 'L' shape from the left side of his mouth across to his ear and up the left side of his nose to his cheek bone. A huge gash ran vertically through his left eyebrow, so close to his eye. I was momentarily riveted to the spot in disbelief, my eyes once more brimming with tears. Somehow, even though I was in shock and my head was spinning, I managed to extricate myself from where I stood without pulling out any of the wires or tubes, and inched my way to the base of the bed to join the others without saying a word.

We were only allowed to spend two minutes with Cayle as he needed to be prepped for surgery.

'Do you want to come back when he is out?' Hazel asked.

'Yes please,' I stammered and, with that, she took down my mobile number.

'Now go back to the apartment and get some rest. We will call you later when he is out of theatre. We have no idea what time that will be.'

'Whatever the time is,' I said, 'we will be back.'

As we numbly walked out of ITU, the image of my son's damaged face was indelibly seared into my memory. We left the hospital in shocked silence.

* * *

That call came at 11.30 pm.

Warrant Officer Armstrong drove back from the hotel where he was staying to pick us up from the apartment and took us across to QEHB. Once again heading upstairs, we went straight to a private waiting room where moments later the consultants joined us to brief us on what they had done.

William Van Niekerk began.

'All of Cayle's wounds have been cleaned and redressed. His face has been stitched back together, and we have done a lot of work around the mouth area.'

'Does he still have his tongue? And have his teeth been damaged? And what about his sight?' The words tumbled out of my mouth. I was astounded when Ian Sargeant replied,

'There appears to be no damage to either his tongue or his teeth. Unfortunately we won't know about his sight until he is conscious. His sinuses have been flushed with three litres of liquid to remove blood and the Afghan grit that was blasted into them, and the ventilation tube has now been wired to Cayle's front teeth to keep it in place.'

After we desperately tried to remember as much as we could, Hazel asked,

'Are you ready to see Cayle?'

We nodded and headed once more down the long and now very quiet corridor to ITU. We sanitised our hands on entering the ward, immediately aware once again of the beeping of various machines. The ward was dimly lit and, after the brightness of the corridor, initially it was hard to know what we were seeing. By the time we reached the area where Cayle was, our eyes had become accustomed to the soft light.

Approaching the bed, we found that the sheet had been dropped to Cayle's waist and a lot more of my son was visible. We were slowly being exposed to the full impact of the blast to his body and there did not seem to be a single area that had not been damaged. Both of his arms were heavily dressed and so was his torso. Cayle had been so shrouded up when we first saw him, and I think that even then I had still been in total denial as to the extent of his injuries. On the car journey up to QEHB, an image had formed in my mind of what Cayle would look like. Coming to terms with the loss of Cayle's legs was going to be hard enough, but I had not even begun to absorb the extent of the other damage done. Nothing was hidden now.

I stood next to the bed on his left-hand side near the bedhead and began scanning my eyes over his body. Recalling the brief we had been given, I glanced at what I knew to be the remains of Cayle's left hand, heavily bandaged but now out from under the cover. I was not prepared for the sight before me. Just from the shape I could tell that the damage was significant. The blood began roaring in my ears, I felt the colour drain from my face and I slumped to the floor. Moments later I came around, aware that I had somehow curled myself up into a tight ball so as not to interfere with any of the equipment keeping my son alive. Hazel came over to help me up and, although sympathetic, she immediately began, 'We're having a tough enough time looking after your son,' she said, 'we do not need to be worrying about you as well. You have to make sure that you all eat, stay hydrated, properly rested and that you support each other. We definitely don't need any added pressure.'

Once I was shakily upright, I glanced over to Seth and noticed that he too was very pale. He staggered towards a chair, flopped down onto it and dropped his head between his knees. Quickly I moved over and knelt down beside him. Tearfully he said, 'I was fine until I held Cayle's hand; it's so cold.'

Reality had started to set in – his big brother was in trouble.

* * *

We left the hospital at about one in the morning, each lost in our own thoughts.

Sitting together drinking tea at the kitchen table in the apartment, the three of us mulled over the barrage of information we had been given, sharing what each of us could remember as I scribbled points into my notebook. An hour later we were all in our beds, although despite Hazel's orders, I don't think any of us got much sleep. I sat up in bed and wrote in my diary while rivers of tears streamed down my cheeks. Turning the bedside light off, I lay down, tossing and turning while constantly going over in my mind the phone calls and messages I had had from Cayle since he'd deployed to Afghanistan. He was having the time of his life and loving every single minute of it. A strict fitness regime and rigorous daily exercise meant that he was in peak physical form, and I prayed that this would stand him in good stead for what lay ahead.

8. Coma

Bronwyn

Throughout the night I constantly leant over to check my phone to make sure that the hospital wasn't trying to get hold of me.

I was so concerned that I might miss a call if I dozed off, and by 5.30 am, after no more than a couple of hours of broken sleep, I decided to get up, shower and sit in the lounge with a cup of coffee. For as long as I could remember I had been a drinker of Rooibos, a South African herbal tea, but it seemed like an appropriate time to change to caffeine, a boost I felt I would need to get me through the day. Before my coffee was finished the boys were up and moving.

'Are we ready for this?' said Rich, knowing that it would be another very long day.

At 10 am, Warrant Officer Armstrong arrived at the apartment to take Seth, Rich and I back to the hospital. Sitting in the back of the car wearing Cayle's body warmer, I found I instinctively reached inside to feel for his tags and I held them in my hand as I wondered what the day would bring.

We headed to one of the consulting rooms and were surprised to find Richard there. He had driven up through France the previous day to catch the last overnight ferry to the UK across the English Channel, arriving at the hospital at about 9.30 am. We greeted and hugged before sitting down to catch up.

Physically and emotionally exhausted from the news and the long drive, he told us:

'I asked at reception where I needed to go and they sent me to ITU. I walked to the ward and pressed the intercom button and said that I was there to see my son, Cayle Royce. They obviously didn't realise that I wasn't with you guys when Cayle was brought in and therefore hadn't seen him, so they just let me in. I looked around the ward for a nurse to ask where I could find him and she pointed me in the direction of his bed. I thought she may escort me to him but she didn't.'

His eyes welled up.

'I only stayed with him for a few minutes because I knew that I needed to come and find you guys.'

We sat down together and between Seth, Rich and I we relayed as much information to Richard as we could remember.

It wasn't long before GC Ian Sargeant came to give us another briefing. It was good for Richard to hear it from the consultant himself.

Only two visitors were allowed to be in Cayle's bed space at a time, so we spent most of the day alternating our visits. The medical staff remarked often on how physically strong Cayle was and how often he had tried to breathe himself, instead of letting the ventilator do the work, which is not something that should have been possible with the amount of sedative he had been given. The purpose of the strong sedative was to prevent him from breathing on his own in order to give his lungs time to heal. However, his body processed the drugs at a phenomenal rate, which resulted in his lungs taking back control from the ventilator.

Due to the extent of his injuries, Cayle had a dedicated nurse with him twenty-four hours a day and he kept them constantly busy.

* * *

After a brief explanation of what it was, I was handed Cayle's patient diary and began flipping through it, immediately becoming very emotional while reading the entries.

8:43 am, 3 May

Roycey, I was there when you got off the MERT. You weren't talking much mate so I came back today to see you off. Worry about nothing mate, we will take care of you and I will personally come and see you wherever you are on my R & R [rest and recreation]. Just think about getting strong, accepting your medal and marching with your fellow soldiers and brothers when we return – your rightful place, mate. Thinking of you and nothing is an ask. RSM [Regimental Sergeant Major] – Sting

8:50 am, 3 May

Hey Joe, came to see you boet. Catch up with you in Birmingham. Rich and Sethy are looking after your Mom. Catch you on the flipside. Roos

10:15 am, 3 May

Royce, you are my best soldier; I have been and will always be unbelievably proud to have served with you. Whatever happens, don't give up. I know you won't because you are made of something else! You are the consummate professional soldier and a damn good man. I am so privileged to have spent so much time with you over the last few years. In particular, I enjoyed getting to know you in Verbier. I expect that in whatever capacity you will achieve excellence in something new. If that turns out to be skiing I promise I will be there for you every step of the way. Good luck, I look forward to seeing you as soon as I get back. In the meantime we'll crack on and you will be an inspiration to me and every man in this troop. Yours, Harry

10:21 am, 3 May

Mate, you are sedated but please know we're standing watch over you. You're one heck of a fighter so please continue to fight. Semper fi. Sgt Maj Tanksley

<u>10:50 am, 3 May</u>

Roycey: I heard you were chatting away throughout and even managed a joke to Troop Leader. You will be missed in the Squadron and I will come visit on R & R. Stay strong. Dalby-Walsh

* * *

We left the hospital that evening with Rich saying, 'Right, we started this morning unsure of whether he would see the day out and he has. We'll take that!'

Back at the accommodation, Richard headed over to the apartment he had been allocated, which was across the field from where we were. The three of us had a group huddle followed by a quick chat over a cup of tea.

'There are so many people wanting to know what's happening and I don't know how to keep everyone informed,' I said, tearfully.

'What about doing one of your email updates every second night and you can send that out to everyone, Ma?' suggested Seth. 'That way you can make sure that nobody gets left out.'

The boys went off to their room and I sat alone at the kitchen table and wrote the following:

Email update: Friday 4 May 2012
On Wednesday Cayle stepped on an improvised explosive device in Afghanistan. Within 31 minutes of the blast he was being airlifted by Chinook helicopter back to Camp Bastion, a 12 minute flight away, where he was immediately taken into the operating theatre. This, together with the instant action of the medic on the ground, saved his life – we were told by one surgeon yesterday that if Cayle had received the same injuries here in the UK he would never have survived because he would not have had the instant medical attention and been taken to

hospital in time. Two Casualty Notification Officers came to deliver the news to me at home on Wednesday evening that Cayle has had a bilateral amputation. They said he had other injuries but they were very vague in explaining them to me. I was told that I would be visited on Thursday morning to be given a further update. Seth immediately drove home from the Royal Marines camp in Beaconsfield to be with me. Yesterday morning we were driven up to Birmingham which is where we are at present. Cayle was back in the UK less than 36 hours after the explosion and he is in THE best hospital in Europe.

Cayle's injuries are severe and he is in a critical condition. This is very graphic so if you are squeamish I suggest you do not read this paragraph. From his head down:

His neck is broken in three places – C3, C6 and C7. At the time of the blast he moved his arms, but he has been heavily sedated since then so the doctors are unsure of the extent of the damage done. He took a lot of the blast to his face and it is in a bad way, especially around his mouth area, but we have been assured that the best maxillofacial surgeon is doing the work on him. The left side of his mouth has been blown open in an 'L' shape from the corner of his mouth to his ear, and up the left side of his nose. His lips have been blown off. He has a gash through his left eyebrow and the fact that he was wearing protective eyewear no doubt saved his eyes. The heat of the blast seared the glasses against his cheeks and the shape of them is clearly visible on his burnt flesh. An ophthalmic surgeon has checked his eyes and apart from a small pressure bubble which will disappear in time, his eyes seem to be fine. His cheekbones are both broken. It is very apparent that he was wearing body armour because where the plates were covering his body, there is little visible damage. The left side of his chest where it meets with his armpit has been blown open where the body armour ends. Both of his biceps have severe shrapnel damage and his lungs are not functioning on their own so he is connected to a ventilator. Cayle has something called blast lung which, even with all of his other visible injuries, seems to have caused the most concern. The impact of the blast caused his lungs to compress at very high speed which has resulted in them being bruised. As with any bruise, the damage will only manifest in a few days' time and this is what the medical staff are very concerned about because the bruising may cause hardening of his lungs. He has a ventilation tube down his throat which has been wired to his front teeth to stop it from moving, plus he has a lot of liquid in his chest cavity. Lung rings have been fitted between his ribs on each side with tubes coming out draining the fluid away. The fingertips of his left hand have been amputated including his thumb, some fingers down one and some two sections. His left inside arm has been stapled closed from his wrist to his elbow. His right femur is broken and the surgeon was going to put a metal plate into it but he has decided to wait on that – introducing a foreign body increases the risk of infection which at this stage is their biggest concern. Both of Cayle's legs have been amputated, the right through the knee and the left below the knee, but there is still quite a lot of Afghan grit in these wounds and they will need to be scrubbed with a hard brush to remove it all. We have been told that there is a big possibility that his legs may have to be amputated higher. He is due to go back for surgery on Sunday to check for any dying tissue as this is also a cause of infection; all his dressings will be changed then. He will remain in an induced coma indefinitely and will slowly be brought out to see how he responds.

But, the positives are: he is still alive, he looks a lot better today and his heart is very strong. We were told yesterday that if they thought that we needed to be at the hospital 24/7 then they would tell us but they have encouraged us to get out of the waiting room as much as possible and to keep ourselves fed and hydrated. The doctors and nursing staff are all totally committed and are talking long term about rehabilitation. This is going to be a long road for all of us, but the support we are receiving is incredible.

Thank you for all your prayers and support.

Bronwyn

* * *

After I had pressed send, I took a moment to reflect. Although I was capable of retaining most of the information we were being fed by the various consultants and I seemed to be able to convey the current situation via email, I was still struggling to accept that the person I had seen lying on the bed was actually my son. The strong young man who in my mind was immortal, now lay broken in a hospital bed.

* * *

Unbeknown to me, the morning after Cayle was injured, Seth had phoned June. June had been married to my late father and we have retained a very close relationship with her; she is like a grandmother to my sons. Unlike my siblings who are all on South African passports and need to apply for visas to travel to the UK, June has an Irish passport and was able to fly over to us immediately. Seth knew that we would need the support.

Cayle's regiment had organised for June to be collected from Heathrow Airport by Sergeant Major John Jarvis and driven directly up to us at the apartment. What we didn't initially know was that John had been nominated by Cayle's regiment as our Visiting Officer (VO) – he would be our link to the military, specifically the Light Dragoons, and assist us wherever necessary. He and Cayle had met briefly on camp before Cayle was deployed to Afghanistan and it was somewhat comforting for me to know that. Even though John had only completed the Casualty Visiting Officer's course two days prior and we were his first assignment, from the moment I met him I felt that he would be the right VO for my family.

After a quick shower and change of clothes, June was ready to come to the hospital with us. We piled into John's car and as he drove, I tried to prepare both him and June mentally for the physical state Cayle was in.

June and I entered ITU, approaching Cayle's bedside without exchanging a word. I heard her quietly gasp. Cayle's heart was beating so powerfully that we could feel the vibration through the steel bed frame. Lost in our own grief, we stood for a few moments and wept. Although he'd been in hospital for a couple of days, dried blood remained visible in places over his body and a constant trickle of fresh blood ran down his left cheek and into his ear. June reached out and stroked his head, feeling the Afghan grit caked to his scalp. She quietly spoke to him and I heard her whisper a prayer. A few minutes with him was more than enough for her to summarise his injuries and, as we left ITU, I could sense the heaviness that she felt.

Back at the hospital restaurant, we met up with Seth, Richard, Rich and John. We were priming John before his first visit to ITU when the Padre came to introduce himself to us. A man of average height and with a very kind face and calm voice, he was new in his role as Military Chaplain at QEHB. I sensed immediately his compassion and understanding, concluding that Jonathon Daniel and I would get on well. His genuine interest and concern shone through and, as he handed me his business card, he made it very clear that he would be available for us whenever we might need him.

That evening, when we went in to say goodnight to Cayle, Richard asked the duty nurse,

'Can I take some photographs of him because I'm sure he'd like to know what he looked like?'

He was strongly advised against it. As we left the ward, I couldn't help but wonder if it was because Cayle wasn't expected to live.

The following morning, June and I were up very early, sitting together in the apartment lounge. We said a few prayers and then talked over a cup of coffee about Cayle and his incident.

'He's just so vulnerable,' June said. 'I wanted to pick him up and hold him but I was almost too scared to touch him because he is so broken.'

'What sort of future will he have when I know that all he ever wants to do is go adventuring?' I said to her with a quaver in my voice. 'I don't even want to think that he may not survive his injuries.'

Words completely escaped her and we sat in silence, each lost in our thoughts. It had been eighteen years since my dad had passed away and I missed him more than ever. I wished he could have been with me but I knew he would be heartbroken at what had happened to his oldest grandchild.

I jumped as my phone rang, jolting me back to reality. It was an early phone call from Claire, the Deputy Critical Care Nurse. 'Cayle has had a good night and is stable enough to undergo surgery. He will be admitted to the operating theatre at 9 am. It's best that you take some time out while you can – stay away from the hospital for a few hours and I will contact you when he is out.'

As a distraction, John drove us into Birmingham to the Bullring Shopping Centre so that we could purchase a few things, including a few items of clothing for me. It had quickly become apparent that three days' worth of clothes was not going to be enough. However, I really struggled with the normality of what was going on around me while my son lay in intensive care fighting for his life. I walked around aimlessly, unable to concentrate on anything, my whole body shaking. I could not stop crying, wanting to shout out to all the faceless people: 'Don't you know what has happened to my child?', but I knew that my own personal crisis would mean nothing to anyone. Rich decided I should stay with Seth, Richard and John at a street cafe. He ordered us coffee and then he went with June to grab a few necessities.

Twice the operating hours were extended when it transpired Cayle's body was stable enough to cope, resulting in more than eight hours of surgery. It had been a very long day for us all, hours of sitting around endlessly in the hospital waiting to hear any morsel of news. Pressure can unveil both the best and the worst in us. The waiting was causing anxiety and stress. Anger seemed to be our constant companion, whether it was at the unfairness of what had happened to Cayle, the apparent way things were being dealt with, or even frustration with each other. There'd been many charged moments as tempers flared, but Padre Jonathon had stuck to his word and was amazing at spending time with each of us, enabling us to offload and calm down.

We were already all very familiar with the route from the restaurant to the hospital chapel. It was on the same level and therefore easily accessible. It became a sanctuary for us. Stepping into the room, a sense of peace was instantly felt among the chaos of our emotional states; it offered somewhere to escape, to reassess. Entering the chapel from the back, rows of wood-framed blue fabric chairs faced towards a wall of floor-to-ceiling windows. Just being able to see the trees and sky outside immediately brought some calm. To the right of the altar, a door led to a smaller counselling room containing a few chairs and it was there that we took turns in spending time chatting to Jonathon.

Early that evening we were called to the consulting room to meet with two of the eight consultants who had operated on Cayle. The general feeling was positive.

LC Al Mountain began: 'Although Cayle is still critical, he is no longer *critical* critical.'

The main purpose of the surgery had been to do a tracheostomy; all the dressings were removed from around his mouth to enable the maxillofacial surgeons to start working on that area. To create some lips for him, the inside of his mouth had been rolled over, sliced and then stitched in place. The surgeon was confident about the reconstruction, assuring us that in time Cayle would be able to talk and eat properly. His right leg had been shortened, resulting in an above-knee amputation. Double above-knee amputation would make it harder for him to walk on prosthetics but it would still be possible. The fingers and thumb of his shattered left hand had been wired to enable the small bones to knit. Unfortunately his index finger had to be completely amputated due to the nerves being destroyed, and trying to save it may have resulted in an infection. The usable underside skin from his index finger had been folded over backwards to close up the tops of his middle and ring fingers, which had been stripped bare by the blast. After further consideration, it had been decided that his right femur needed stabilising and a metal rod, screws and pins had been inserted.

After the update we were offered the opportunity of spending some time with Cayle. Moments later, June and I were walking towards his bed when we saw that the curtains had been pulled aside. I caught a glimpse of him and my heartbeat increased rapidly as I approached the bedside. Still under the effects of the anaesthetic, and although his face was extremely swollen, it was possible to see some of the Cayle we knew.

I reached out to take his right hand in mine with incredible heaviness in my heart.

'I'm so sorry, my child.'

June and I held onto each other and wept.

'No mother should have to witness this,' she whispered.

Back at the apartment that evening, we realised that a lot of positives could be taken from the day and we chose to focus on those. The encouraging and optimistic attitudes of all the medical staff and surgeons helped us move forward.

* * *

Over the following couple of days, Cayle was deemed stable enough to have the sedation reduced. He was being fed via a tube through his nose and on one occasion I was standing alongside his bed when he got hiccups. It reminded me of being pregnant with him – I'd loved it when he hiccupped because it was a sign of the little life growing inside of me.

We started to see small but encouraging things happening – Cayle would blink his right eye when drops were put into his left eye. Although still connected to the ventilator, he was breathing on his own. As soon as we started to speak to him, he tried to open his eyes. He immediately got agitated and, being a physically strong lad, he started moving about. It disturbed me greatly, just the thought that he may be in pain but couldn't tell us. Distressing as it was to watch, this of course proved that he was not paralysed, which was fantastic news. Thankfully the hospital staff had had the foresight to fit a neck brace to prevent further damage.

I called Seth in to join me and he stood holding Cayle's hand. 'He's squeezing it,' Seth said with a grin on his face.

* * *

A week to the day after Cayle's incident, Betty phoned me. It was the first time we had spoken since she'd packed the carrier bag with my belongings for what I'd thought would be three days away. After asking after Cayle, she added, 'Love, I've been approached by the local media to give a statement – what should I do?'

I became instantly enraged.

'What right do they have to contact you?' I asked in disbelief. 'He is fighting for his life and we don't want this to be splashed all over the media! Thank you for letting me know, Betty – I'll get it dealt with.'

I was so angry at the apparent insensitivity of the reporter. It made me think back to when the officers had come to my flat to deliver the news to me and how they'd warned me that this may happen.

Overhearing my conversation, Rich stepped aside and made a phone call. Moments later he came over to me and very quietly said, 'It's been taken care of, Mom.'

I still have no idea who he spoke to, but we never heard from the media again in all the time we spent at the hospital.

* * *

Cayle constantly had a high temperature and a towel was regularly being soaked in a bucket of ice and water and then draped across his body – it was incredibly harrowing to watch as, despite being in a coma, he understandably gasped each time. His sedation had been switched on and off over a few days depending on how he was deemed to be coping.

One particular day it was off and it seemed as though he had started to respond to our voices. I leant forward and with tears trickling down my cheeks, I whispered in his ear, 'I wish I could take some of the pain away from you.'

He began thrashing around in the bed. Startled, I jumped backwards. I felt as though my heart was going to break into a million pieces – never have I ever experienced anything like it. To try to ease the anxiety, some of us had taken to stroking his head in an attempt to calm him down. It was also a way of making physical contact with him as there was very little of him that we could touch. That particular day it did not help.

The passing days brought other dynamics as understandably nerves were frayed and emotions were continually running high, each of us dealing with our angst in a different way. Group morale was very low and I was doing my best to outwardly seem in control, while inside I was in turmoil. Richard, struggling with the helplessness he felt, was more vocal, occasionally letting off steam.

We were taking turns in spending a bit of much-needed quiet time in the chapel. I had had a particularly bad day and Jonathon sat with me, giving me a chance to chat and offload a few things. I am prone to take things way too personally and I was under the impression that Richard was upset with me because I was always the one who the doctors or medical staff contacted or consulted first. I later found out from Richard that he was pleased that I was the hub or the go-to person because I was more approachable and communicable in the situation, whereas he was far more volatile and explosive.

When we left the hospital that evening, Cayle was asleep and he looked slightly more at peace.

Back at the apartment and once the others had gone to bed, I sat down at the kitchen table, put my head in my hands and began to weep softly. I realised that we would definitely be needing some help in the future. I reached into my handbag and pulled out a business card that I had tucked away in my purse. I emailed the person who had given it to me.

I had met Emma Parry three months prior while I was working at a Home and Gift trade fair in Birmingham. A tall woman with a mop of beautiful auburn curls, when she came onto the stand enquiring about greetings cards, I was instantly drawn to her. I didn't realise who she was but we struck up a conversation and from something she said, I understood that somehow she was linked to the military. I mentioned to her that I had two sons who were serving, both of them due to deploy to Afghanistan later in the year, one in March and the other in August. She told me she too had a son in the military, so she knew how stressful it could be. Offering me her business card, she encouraged me to contact her any time I needed support. She'd exuded such kindness and I felt an immediate rapport with her. As she walked away, I glanced down at the card in my hand and realised that she was Emma Parry, co-founder of Help for Heroes, a British military charity launched in 2007 to help provide better facilities for British servicemen and women who have been wounded or injured in the line of duty. This felt like more than a chance meeting.

* * *

The day was now Thursday, 10 May, and it was hard to believe that it had been a week since I had first laid eyes on my son's shattered body.

The endless minutes had dragged but the week itself had somehow sped by. So much had happened and yet there had been hours and hours of what seemed to be interminable nothing. It had also been one week since I first slipped on Cayle's body warmer and been handed his dog tags; I had worn both every day since.

Cayle's surgery due that morning had been postponed until the afternoon, which gave June time to say farewell to him – she would be boarding a plane back to South Africa that evening. As we stood beside his bed, I watched how tender she was with him, having no idea when or even if she would see him again.

She spoke gently: 'Don't give up fighting, Cayle. I'm sorry I cannot stay with you until you are awake but your family are here with you and I'll be keeping you in my prayers.'

She and I walked out of ITU together, arms linked, and I sensed the heaviness she was feeling.

Back in the restaurant lounge area, we hugged and said our farewells. 'Thank you for coming over to support us,' I said. 'You have been a pillar of strength to all of us. I know it has not been easy but we are so grateful that you have been here.'

Rich and Seth drove June down to Heathrow Airport, while Richard and I remained at the hospital. Cayle was taken into theatre yet again where all of his dressings were changed and more work was done on his face. When we saw him a few hours later, a decision had been made to leave him sedated until the morning. After kissing him goodnight, we headed back to our respective apartments for an early night.

Seated once again at the kitchen table, I realised that I would have a few hours completely alone for the first time since receiving the news of Cayle's incident. Knowing that Rich and Seth would be back from the airport later that night, I took the opportunity to open up my notebook and iPad and busy myself with catching up on emails. In my inbox was a heartfelt response from Emma.

Dear Bronwyn

I am devastated to hear about your son. It must be unimaginably awful for you and your family and I am so, so sorry to hear that he's been wounded in this way. We have met many young men like Cayle in hospital who, two or three years down the line, are doing incredible things and learning more about themselves than they would have ever imagined. I have no doubt that he will make a full recovery but it is still really hard for you, as his mother, to come to terms with this.

Please keep in touch and let me know how Cayle is doing. I know he is getting the very best care at QEHB; you, as his mum, need support too, and we will do everything we can to help with this.

With best wishes
Emma Parry

* * *

The following day the Colonel of the Light Dragoons, Major General Andrew Stewart, was driven down from camp to the hospital. Tall in stature, utterly professional, and the epitome of a man of his rank, I was pleased to meet him and very grateful that he had spared us his time. Realising that I was unsure of how to address him, he said, 'Please, call me Andrew.' And that instantly put me at ease.

Seth, however, continued to call him 'Sir'.

Andrew spent a long time chatting to Richard, Seth and myself in one of the waiting rooms, enquiring about what could be done to ease our situation, offering assistance wherever possible. That done, he asked if we could take him to see Cayle. Recognising Andrew's rank, when Seth sought permission from the DCCN for three of us instead of two to enter ITU, it was quickly granted.

As we approached Cayle's bed I couldn't help but notice that Andrew had to reach out to hold onto the nurse's station to steady himself. His face was ashen and he was clearly momentarily lost for words. He managed to compose himself and expressed his sincere condolences. Perhaps as a distraction, he directed the conversation towards matters more practical. Seth mentioned a few issues, one of them being the fact that Cayle had been in the UK for six years yet still did not have a British passport.

'We are unsure of how this will affect him regarding medical and other issues going forward,' Seth said.

Andrew promised to look into it for us and when he left the hospital an hour later he assured us that he would be back.

That evening, when Richard and I went to say goodnight to Cayle, we were asked by one of the nurses to bring in a recent photograph of him, which would be placed on the nurses' stand at the end of his bed. It would be as important for the medical staff as for us. We chose one of him taken by the resident Padre on camp out in Afghanistan a few days before he was injured.

* * *

Days of consistently trying to bring Cayle's temperature down and his blood pressure up meant that my son had so many holes in him that he was starting to look like a pin cushion. The dressing from his right bicep had been removed and it was the first time I had actually seen the size of the wound, made larger by the surgeon's attempt to remove some of the shrapnel. Being told by Ian Sargeant that if the wound had been 3 or 4 mm deeper Cayle's arm would have had to be amputated didn't bear thinking about.

Seth:

I remember going into ITU when Cayle was still physically strong, which would have been maybe a week or two in. Both of his arms were heavily bandaged but his right hand was free. I walked into the ward and as I came around the corner to where Cayle's bed was, there was a nurse being lifted off the ground by him. She had been trying to push his arm down onto the bed to make him more comfortable but he was lifting her straight up, her feet dangling off the ground. With wide eyes and a trembling voice she said, 'He's really strong', and I went, 'Yeah, he is pretty strong – do you want a hand?'

I think they doubled his sedatives then – they realised quite quickly that he processed drugs like a heroin addict.

* * *

'Hurry up and wait ....' – something we had heard and experienced many times over the previous days. The waiting continued, seemingly without end. Cayle was due to have surgery, but he had developed a lung infection and his left lung was filled with fluid. He was back on a ventilator and he needed a CT scan but was in a queue due to more injured soldiers having been brought in from Afghanistan.

It was heartbreaking watching the new families coming through, their perilous journeys just beginning. I felt incredible compassion and wanted to reach out to comfort them, eager to assist in any way. When Jonathon approached me about being available for them, I was more than willing to offer them some support. In this way I was in fact encouraging myself by comprehending how far we had come in our journey with Cayle.

The results of the CT scan revealed that he had a lot of blood lying around the chest rings. The current rings needed removing and new ones inserted, but that had to wait until his temperature came down. Surgery was booked for a few days later. In the meantime it had been decided to move him to a private room that had natural daylight.

I spent some time at his bedside, with the sunlight gently falling across his skin, marvelling at the miracle of the human body. His face had tinges of purple and yellow where the bruising was coming out. It was shocking to see just how close he had come to losing his left eye and, in the bright light, the silvery scars from the glasses seemed more pronounced. His head continued to swell, a result of the increased movement of fluid and white blood cells into the injured area. His neck brace had to be exchanged for a larger one. Some of the dressings had been removed from Cayle's right arm, exposing his bicep, which had a sentry line of staples holding it together. His left arm remained hidden under dressings while dangling raised in a sling in an attempt to reduce the swelling.

He was not off the critical list but things were moving slowly in the right direction.

Watching him lying comatose in the hospital bed, my mind wandered back to our backpacking trip around Greece and Italy. Immense gratitude washed over me that we had seized that opportunity to travel together and for the time we had shared.

* * *

A few days after Cayle had been injured, we'd begun setting up every morning in the relaxation area of the restaurant, which consisted of padded armchairs and coffee tables, dragging chairs from nearby to increase the circle as more people joined us. The medical staff and welfare officers all knew exactly where to find us and we nicknamed our spot 'FOB Royce'. The definition of a FOB (Forward Operating Base) is 'any secured forward military position, commonly a military base used to support tactical operations. The base may be used for an extended period of time.' This name seemed very appropriate for us.

It was now mid-May and Cayle was having a couple of stable days. He opened his eyes regularly and even seemed to smile occasionally. His eye colour had changed from beautiful ice blue to a hazy grey, which I assumed was from the shock of the incident and the impact of the blast to his body.

I was with him one day, chatting away while his eyes focused on me.

'I love you so much and I have missed you. I can't wait to have a proper chat,' I said, feeling as though my heart would overflow with love for this child of mine.

My bubble was burst when the nurse leaned over and quietly said, 'He will never recall any of this – the drugs will prevent him from remembering.'

Although I found it hard to believe, it was not the first time we had been told this.

9. Setback

Bronwyn
17 May 2012

We had passed the two-week mark. We had started to think that things were stable, then the day started with a jolt.

My phone sprang to life before 8 am, just as I was climbing out of the shower. I reached down to the bathroom floor to pick it up and saw that it was a call from the DCCN.

'Bronwyn, Cayle has taken a bad turn and we need you at the hospital immediately. He struggled overnight. His chest has deteriorated and the infection is in both of his lungs. He is relying totally on the ventilator.'

'Claire, we will be there as soon as possible.'

Shocked and shaking, I phoned Richard to tell him. I then banged on the boys' bedroom door to give them the news. We had all lulled ourselves into believing that Cayle was well on the road to recovery and now this.

Richard was over with us in fifteen minutes and Rich raced us across to the hospital. We ran up the stairs to find Claire, who had organised a meeting with Dr Sinclair and LC Mountain. Once again we found ourselves seated in the counselling room, where then followed a report on Cayle's current state.

The bruising to his lungs meant that he had not been breathing deeply enough for the gas exchange (of incoming oxygen and outgoing carbon dioxide) to take place. This had caused a build-up of fluid in his lungs, and in fact a build-up of fluid in his whole body. With him being 'very, very, very ill' (doctor's words), he was not managing to expel it; his lungs were literally soaked. An ultrasound had revealed that the right side of Cayle's heart was also not functioning because of bruising. After much debate, it was decided to link him to a dialysis machine in an attempt to extract at least 150 ml of fluid per hour from his blood. This process could take a few days, depending on how he responded. His temperature was extremely high at 39.8 degrees and one way to reduce this was to cool the blood. The tubes from the dialysis machine were placed in a bucket of cold water and ice. His blood circulating through the tubes would pass through the icy water before it went back into his body. There was a risk that the dialysis machine could affect his kidneys, but Dr Sinclair was sure they would recover with time.

'Unfortunately there is no textbook to refer to when it comes to healing lungs,' she said. 'Cayle has tried to override the ventilator with his own breathing a few times, so he has been heavily sedated to paralyse him so the ventilator can do all the work for him. His stomach has been pumped to remove any bile or feed in case he vomits, which could result in it entering his lungs, causing further problems.'

After a lengthy session with the consultants, I wanted to see Cayle for myself. Rich and I were the first to enter ITU and we found that he had again been moved, this time to be closer to the nurses' station. It was hard to comprehend what we had just been told. Externally, Cayle looked just the same as he had the day before; the difference was the number of machines surrounding his bed. He seemed to have more wires connected to him than the National Grid. I'd started to be able to interpret some of the jargon on the screens of the equipment he was surrounded by and my eyes scanned over them as I neared his bed.

Rich and I stood with the DCCN while she explained their various functions. The news we had just been given, together with the sight of all the new equipment, was enough to tip Rich over the edge. Out of the corner of my eye I noticed him sway as he began to feel faint. The colour drained from his face and he stumbled across to a chair before flopping down onto it.

I walked over to him and put my hand on his shoulder.

'How is this possible, Mom?' He was completely choked up and shaking, not wanting to believe that after all this time Cayle could still be so critical. 'I thought he was well on his way to getting better. How much more can his body take?'

Talking to Dr Sinclair that evening as we stood beside Cayle's bed, she told me, 'If any of my staff tell you they understand what you are going through, please report them to me because they don't know what they are talking about.'

She continued, 'I am trying to put myself in your position; what would I do if it was my son – would I move him to another hospital somewhere else in the world? No, I wouldn't. I honestly believe that this is *the* best hospital Cayle could be in. I have access to every doctor or physician needed for Cayle's current situation and I will call on them whenever I need to.'

That seemed more than enough confirmation for me and I thanked her.

Two days later, and although Cayle was still 'critical, critical', things had slowly started to improve. We had a chat with Dr Van Niekerk outside of ITU and he informed us that the dialysis machine was drawing fluids as it was intended to and that Cayle had continued to urinate – these were promising signs that there would be no detrimental effect on his kidneys.

* * *

With visitors' visas finally in their passports, two of my sisters, Janice and Michelle, landed at Heathrow Airport from South Africa early on the morning of 20 May. They were collected from the airport by a member of the Light Dragoons and driven up to meet us at the apartment.

They were barely over the threshold before we group-hugged and shed a couple of tears. Setting their bags aside, we gathered around the kitchen table to share a pot of tea and catch up on the latest news. After a non-stop twelve-hour flight followed by a two-and-a-half-hour drive, they were tired and emotional, but anxious to see for themselves how we were coping.

Showered and refreshed, we were at the hospital in time for 11 am visiting hours. My sisters had not seen Cayle since June 2006 when he'd left South Africa to join the British military. These were not the circumstances we would have foreseen for a reunion.

I had sought permission from the DCCN for the three of us to see him together. As we approached his bed, I was instantly relieved to notice that the dialysis machine and the nitric oxide ventilators had done their duties and had been removed from Cayle's bed-space; it was less for the girls to have to take in. With their eyes scanning over Cayle's body and the plethora of equipment surrounding him, a few minutes was more than enough for them each to have a moment to speak gently to him and to reassure him that they were there.

They were both rather quiet as we left ITU and entered the corridor, each processing things in their own way. Sitting down in FOB Royce, Janice tearfully spoke up: 'I'm struggling with the image of the sheet just falling away where it should have been covering Cayle's legs.'

My thoughts fled back to the very first instant I had laid eyes on his broken body. How uncanny that she and I had had the exact same thoughts.

Trying to be positive, Michelle said, 'He looks so much better than I expected him to. Let's try to focus on the good things.' I know my sister well, however, and I wondered what was really going through her head.

Later in the day on my way back from the ward, I met one of the consultants in the corridor. 'We've switched some of Cayle's sedatives off and reduced others. It may take some time but he could start coming out of his coma soon,' she told me. 'We need to closely monitor him though, so please don't expect too much.'

That evening before we left the hospital, we went to see him. Cayle opened his eyes and started to look around the room. What joy to see his eyes open again and I was delighted that my sisters could share this time with us. Cayle seemed quite peaceful despite shuffling around a bit in the bed. Claire, the DCCN, spoke to him, asking him to raise his eyebrows or blink if he understood her. Although it took him a few moments, he mostly responded.

Kissing the top of his head, I said goodnight and began to walk away with a new lightness in my step.

Claire called after me: 'Bronwyn, it's great to see how well Cayle is doing. Please just be aware that he has had a lot of sedation over the past three weeks, so he may not remember any of this.'

I nodded as I bid her goodnight and walked away.

Unexpectedly, and because Cayle had had a stable night and his lungs were the best they had been for a long while, the following day the surgeons decided to use this window of opportunity to operate. The procedures included a large skin graft taken from his right thigh and attached to his left elbow, left hand and thumb, and stump of left leg. He'd also had yet another chest X-ray to determine the placement of certain tubes and to check on the chest drains. By this time we had lost count of the number of blood transfusions he had had, but the medical staff all seemed very happy with his progress, giving lots of thumbs-ups.

When we eventually saw Cayle, the anaesthetic had worn off and he seemed a bit agitated. Unfortunately, due to his broken neck and the poor state of his lungs, he had not been regularly turned and as a result it was found that he had developed pressure sores on the back of his head and lower back. A smaller one was starting to form on his chin from the rubbing of the neck brace. We suspected that these sores were what was causing his discomfort.

Hearing that he was out of theatre, Matron Teresa Griffiths joined us. She was as surprised as we were to find his eyes were open.

'Cayle, are you in any pain?' she asked him. He shook his head.

Turning to us, she went on, 'If any of us had been given even a tenth of the sedation he had, we would be completely knocked out. He has the constitution of an elephant!'

She continued, 'And as for responding, we are amazed that he seems to be understanding us, although we don't expect he will remember this.'

Cayle seemed far more alert when we saw him the next day. The duty nurse knew the signs and he told us that Cayle was hallucinating, one of the side effects of the huge amount of drugs administered. His eyes were wide open yet he seemed very fearful. As his mother, this was disturbing to watch because I wanted to shield him from it all. He had been so protective of me over the years and yet now when he needed me, I was helpless. I could not stop the tears from spilling over.

10. 50/50

Bronwyn
23 May 2012
Day 22

A constant and ongoing concern was that Cayle's bowels had not worked at all since his incident three weeks earlier. All the opioids, including morphine, had contributed to extreme constipation. Despite laxatives and even an enema, nothing had helped. I was standing alongside his bed when David the duty nurse asked,

'Cayle, do you have any pain?' Cayle nodded.

'Can you show me where the pain is?' asked David, and very slowly Cayle lifted his right hand and reached for his lower abdomen.

David recognised that immediate action was required. An X-ray was done to alleviate the possibility of bowel blockages or damage. Thankfully that was clear. We were told that it was only a matter of time before the laxatives Cayle had been given would begin to work.

On 23 May a medical decision was taken to stop all of Cayle's sedation; it was an emotionally charged day all around. He was still heavily drugged, and we were assured once again that he would have little or no recollection of the day; more than likely, no recollection of anything from the moment of the blast.

Right from when I first laid eyes on Cayle that morning, I knew it would be a toughie. I went to say hello to him and he turned his head to look at me. I leant forward to kiss his forehead, he picked his head up to meet me ... and we both cried. He was extremely agitated and thrashed around. I was thankful for the neck brace he still wore. The nurse was having a hard time keeping him on the bed. It was difficult to know how much he was comprehending and how much he remembered about what had happened to him. I held his hand but I found it all greatly upsetting, and pleaded with her to do something for him. Her advice was for us to visit him as little as possible during the day while she tried to balance his medication.

When I saw Cayle early that evening, he was asleep, looking a little more peaceful. He'd been rolled onto his side, which meant that the pressure sores on his head and back had some relief. However, he had been re-sedated because there was concern that he might fall off the bed due to how much he flailed around.

As I was leaving his bedside, I thanked the nurse on duty.

'I won't need to go to the gym for a few weeks after the workout he has given me today!' she responded with a little giggle. She looked exhausted.

It never ceased to amaze me just how dedicated the staff were.

Another two days passed and Cayle's non-working tummy had now become seriously problematic. Something desperately needed to be done. The X-ray had shown no blockages, so a CT scan was ordered, followed by an urgent meeting with Dr Sinclair, LC Mountain, GC Sargeant and ourselves.

Richard, Janice, Michelle and I sat anxiously in the consulting room. As always, Dr Sinclair was very straight-talking,

'Cayle's lungs continue to be a huge concern because of the damage done by the blast,' she said. 'He has little reserve in his lungs, so he is working hard to keep his body going. His temperature is constantly very high and the cause has not been established. On top of all of this is the huge concern that Cayle's bowels are so distended that they are now pushing up against his lungs, further restricting them. I have called for the advice of a bowel specialist, who is due to look at the scan results.'

GC Ian Sargeant interjected, 'Cayle is critically ill. He still has only a 50/50 chance of survival.'

I sharply drew breath. It had felt as though someone had physically punched me in the guts. In that split second I'd feared my child may die. That was the first and only time since the moment I had found out about Cayle's injuries that I had doubted whether he would survive. He was clinging to life by a thread.

Dr Sinclair added, 'Cayle is very, very, very critical, but he is still fighting. No human should have survived these injuries.'

Ian added, 'We are not designed to be this ill for this long.'

Cayle's incredible fitness was undoubtedly playing a major role in his survival, but no one knew if it would be enough.

I thanked them for the update. Dazed, we left the room in silence. Shaken and stunned, the girls headed back to the restaurant, and Richard and I along the corridor to ITU to see Cayle. He was very heavily sedated and completely unresponsive. I held his right hand in mine and began to weep inconsolably. The helplessness was like nothing any of us had ever experienced; we were nearing breaking point.

Richard left the bedside and approached DCCN Matt, enquiring as to when the specialist would be arriving, only to be informed that because it was now Friday afternoon, he wouldn't be in until Monday. It was too much for Richard and he completely saw red.

In a fit of rage and out of concern for his son, he shouted at Matt, 'This is totally unacceptable! You get hold of Dr Sinclair immediately and tell her that if the specialist is not in the hospital by tonight, I will personally go to the head of the hospital and cause a scene.'

I felt pity for Matt being at the receiving end of the outburst, but I was not surprised by Richard's reaction.

Unnerved by the confrontation, Matt contacted Dr Sinclair. Richard was summoned to her office and, with heightened tempers from both of them, she told him that she could not have him confronting her staff in such a manner and that if he persisted, she would have him banned from the hospital. She told him that Cayle was her top priority and that she was doing her very best to ensure that the problem was dealt with the utmost urgency. The scan result had been sent to the specialist and she was awaiting instruction.

Richard had stormed out of her office and back to the restaurant. We could clearly see that there must have been a confrontation. Without saying a word, he picked up his belongings and walked out of the hospital. It wasn't long before Padre Jonathon came over to us.

'Have you seen Richard?' he enquired.

'He was here a few minutes ago but he took his things and left the hospital without saying anything,' said Janice.

'Is everything okay?'

Jonathon explained that he had bumped into Dr Sinclair in the ward when she was checking up on Cayle. Knowing that Jonathon had a good relationship with us, she had relayed to the padre that there had been an incident between herself and Richard and she asked if he would check in with us.

'I am very concerned about Richard,' said Jonathon.

'He must have walked back to his accommodation,' I responded.

Wherever he had gone, I hoped that the walk would help him to calm down.

* * *

Before I left the hospital that evening, I went back into the ward and I was relieved to hear that Cayle's bowels had started to work. I expressed my relief and Matt replied, 'The specialist prescribed rocket fuel!' We both smiled.

Although it was only liquid that Cayle was passing, the fact that something was happening was enough reason to celebrate. Even Colin the nurse seemed pleased – and he had to clean it up!

In an early update call the following morning, I was told that Cayle had had a stable night and that we should leave the staff to get on with him for the morning. It gave us much-needed time to get out for a long walk and enjoy being in the fresh air and sunshine.

On entering ITU later that day, Richard and I found Cayle to be quite alert as his sedation had been dropped again. He was off the ventilator and breathing through bellows. He appeared to be far more comfortable and although his eyes remained closed most of the time, he seemed to be semi-aware of things going on around him.

Ian Sargeant came by on his rounds. After a brief update, Richard asked, 'Can I tell Cayle the extent of his injuries? I want him to hear it from me.'

'Richard, although he may appear alert, I doubt very much that he will have any understanding or memory of what you say, but you go ahead,' Ian said as he left us alone.

Richard began to speak gently to Cayle, describing every injury in detail. As he went on, Cayle became increasingly agitated and tears trickled down his cheeks. I was kissing his forehead in the hopes of calming him but he became more and more distressed. Eventually the duty nurse asked us to leave so that she could settle him.

That evening before we left the hospital, we stopped in to see Cayle. He was back on the ventilator for the night and had been sedated again to ensure he got some rest. Thus the peaks and troughs of his recovery continued.

Taking the following morning off to do chores, at lunchtime I received a call from a very excited Padre Jonathon: 'Dr Sinclair wants you here as soon as possible. Cayle appears to be alert and she feels you should be here with him.'

Twenty minutes later when Richard and I got to ITU, Jonathon was at Cayle's bedside chatting to him and Cayle appeared to be conscious of what was happening around him. The nurse told us that his sedation had once again been switched off but that he was not fully cognisant. He was following everyone with his eyes and he turned his head to look when various sounds were made. Cayle had nodded at us when we approached but, as his mother, I could see the haunting fear in his eyes. He did appear to smile though when Jonathon ordered him to 'get better soon because I'm waiting to take you downstairs to Costa for a coffee because the coffee up here is shit!'

I noticed that Cayle's eyes didn't seem to be as milky as the last time I had seen them open, although they were still a murky grey. They were very wide open and he was gesturing with his head towards things and we were explaining as best we could what they were for. As the moments ticked by, he got more and more agitated, distressed and anxious, and whenever we let go of his hand he would grasp out to try to hold onto us. I couldn't help but feel there was more going on in his head than we had presumed. He seemed particularly concerned about the clock on the pillar suspended above his bed. I tried to pacify him as Jonathon explained, 'It's just a clock, Cayle, and the wires coming down from the sockets in the pillar are for the machines around you.'

Before our eyes, Cayle was fast deteriorating and becoming more and more overwrought and no amount of reassurance seemed to help. The nurse stepped forward and said, 'I think he is hallucinating and I need to give him some attention. I'm going to have to ask you to please leave.'

When we walked out of the ward thirty minutes after arriving, Cayle was sopping wet from sweat and the nurses had to do a bed change.

We went to say goodnight to him that evening and were disappointed to find that he had been sedated again, taken off the bellows and put back onto the ventilator.

'After you left, Cayle slept for the rest of the afternoon – he clearly found the whole experience quite traumatic,' said the nurse.

Feeling completely drained, I left the ward, Seth following closely behind me. We walked down the corridor, his arm resting heavily across my shoulder, my head leaning against his chest. There was no need for words.

It had been a week since we'd last seen our VO, John. He drove down from camp to spend the morning with us, excited to see Cayle's progress. He and I were the first to head to the ward, only to be disappointed when we got to his bedside to find Cayle totally sedated. The nurse told us, 'He struggled during the night and his breathing became very erratic. It was decided to leave him sedated for his own safety.'

After a quick update with John before he went back to camp, we were all feeling down and disheartened, so Rich suggested we get away from the hospital for a few hours. A change of scenery in Solihull would do us all good. I still dreaded being away from the hospital and was always anxious, constantly needing to check my phone to make sure it had reception. We'd barely been in Solihull for ten minutes when I felt my phone vibrating in my pocket. It was the DCCN:

'Bronwyn, Cayle has taken a bad turn – can you come in as soon as possible as Dr Torlinski would like to see you.'

All our hearts sank as we ran back to the car and Rich sped us across to QEHB. We were each lost in our own thoughts and filled with trepidation; I sat crippled with tears and totally unable to believe that yet again we'd gone from mountain top to valley bottom. Janice gently touched my arm in support. I phoned Richard to tell him to meet us at the hospital.

Leaving the others in the car, Seth and I ran up the stairs and along the corridor where we met Richard at the door into ITU. We entered together and when I saw that Cayle had been connected to yet another machine, this one being the biggest and noisiest we had seen, I was overcome with sorrow.

Dr Tomasz Torlinski stood at Cayle's bedside. He introduced himself as a critical care consultant and began explaining, 'Cayle's breathing has deteriorated. His lungs were instantly compressed with the impact of the blast. The bruising has caused his lungs to harden, therefore making it very difficult for him to breathe. He is not getting enough oxygen and the erratic breathing is causing him more harm. We've made a decision to completely sedate and paralyse him so that the oscillator does the breathing for him. Taking him off the ventilator and connecting him to the oscillator will ensure that his lungs have the best chance of recovering.'

Cayle looked peaceful as he was being constantly gently shaken by the action of the machine. The vibration was loosening the mucus in his chest and it was being manually suctioned as opposed to waiting for him to cough on his own and then having it suctioned. He was being tended by two ITU nurses around the clock. It was expected that he would be on the oscillator for about three days.

The medical see-saw had tipped again. It had been almost four weeks since he had been injured and I hadn't expected a setback of this magnitude. As I walked away from Cayle's bedside, I felt as though I had no more tears to cry. I wondered how much more his body could take before giving up. Physical and emotional exhaustion was certainly taking its toll on me.

Dr Torlinski had told us not to expect quick results and he was right.

During my regular early morning phone call, I was told by the DCCN that Cayle had had another bad night.

We rushed to the hospital and found him looking much the same as he had the day before; it was something I continually struggled with. Apart from the visible wounds and scars, which would be with him for the rest of his life, it was hard to comprehend that in fact there was still far more going on inside his body that we needed to be concerned about.

Dr Torlinski approached, gently reassuring us. I asked him for an explanation of the purpose of the oscillator and got his version of 'Oscillators for Dummies', which really helped.

'High-frequency oscillation ventilation differs from conventional ventilation in that very small breaths are delivered very rapidly (180 to 900 breaths per minute). This helps with the opening of collapsed lung tissue by providing constant positive pressure in a person's airway while holding the lungs in a paralysed state. The machine is totally replacing his lung function.'

What I did find exceptionally interesting was that there had been no less than eight official explanations of how an oscillator actually works,

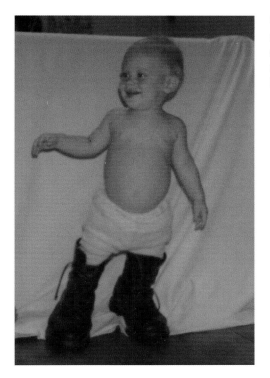

Cayle, a 10-month-old future adventurer, trying on Richard's army boots – a picture that would find its place on our fridge during his deployment to Afghanistan.

Childhood memories forged on a South African farm with his trusty companion, Buddy.

2005: On a journey through Greece and Italy, a mother–son duo creating memories to last a lifetime.

October 2005: Cayle, 19, on the summit of Mount Kilimanjaro, Africa's highest and the world's tallest free-standing mountain.

The final frame before deployment, March 2012: From left to right – Gerhard Roos, Seth, Rich Baker, and Cayle.

Camp Bastion Chronicles, April 2012: Roos, Andy Couling, and Cayle.

Amongst the poppy fields of Afghanistan.

The calm before the storm: 1st May 2012, a day prior to Cayle's life-altering incident.

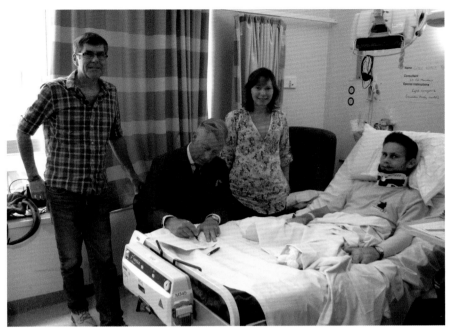

First brush with royalty: Prince Charles visits wounded soldiers, including Cayle, in Queen Elizabeth Hospital Birmingham, June 2012.

Braving a chilly December day for the Light Dragoons medals ceremony, Dereham, Norfolk.

August 2013: The grand foyer of the Grosvenor Hotel, London, serving as the backdrop for Bronwyn's Good Housekeeping magazine's photoshoot. Courtesy of Hearst Magazines UK.

December 2013, La Gomera: Richard's engineering skills coming in handy for seat adaptations during the preparations for the first Atlantic Ocean crossing.

January 2014: A victorious moment captured as the team crosses the finishing line in Antigua, 48 days after setting off. Photo credit Ben Duffy.

Cherishing a triumphant moment: Front left to right – Cayle, Mark Jenkins, Scott Blaney. Rear left to right – Shorty (Sgt James Short), James Kayll, David Scammel.

Royal rendezvous: Cayle explaining the workings of the boat to Prince Harry at a medals ceremony at the River and Rowing Museum, Henley-on-Thames, Oxfordshire.

Bond of Brotherhood. Photo credit Sophie Bolesworth.

when in fact nobody was 100 per cent clear. It was even referred to as a 'God Machine'. There is only one tube into the lungs, yet the oxygen goes in and the carbon dioxide comes out of the same tube without mixing.

He smiled when he said, 'In 100 years' time engineers will probably laugh at the oscillator and the clumsiness of it, but for now it is the best thing available.'

* * *

Ten days after first seeing Cayle, my sister Michelle finally broke down. Since she had arrived at the hospital, I'd felt that outwardly she had appeared far too strong. She was standing alongside the bed looking at her nephew while holding his right hand, and all it took was the gentle words from the nurse working at the bed next to Cayle's to set her off; she could no longer contain her grief and the floodgates opened. It was good for Michelle to be able to release all her pent-up emotions, but it took the rest of the day for her to stabilise. Thankfully we had not all reached our emotional limit on the same day and we were able to encourage her with how far Cayle had come.

The previous day I had asked a few people to pray for a miraculous healing of Cayle's lungs. Gemma, the nurse on duty that afternoon, was standing on the right side of Cayle's bed and I was on the left. She was putting drops into his eyes; I had my hand on his chest, as I often did, and was quietly praying. All of a sudden the alarm on the oscillator went off … and Cayle started to move. Gemma and I both leapt in fright, a combination of his unexpected movement and the really loud alarm.

Gemma gasped, 'He's trying to breathe! It shouldn't be possible with the amount of sedation he's been given!'

Then he did it again.

She called out for permission to increase his sedation, which she received. She administered it and we smiled at each other with relief. Moments later the alarm went off and Cayle's chest moved as he inhaled again. The nurses were astounded. Yet again the sedation was increased and he settled down. It was back to the chuff-chuffing of the oscillator, although I have to confess that when I left the ward I was proudly thinking, 'That's my boy!'

* * *

It was now the beginning of June. The changing of the seasons from spring to summer was clear and the sun began to split the trees in the early hours of the morning. For us, it was more of the same, except that Rich had left us to take his family on a planned holiday to Disneyland. He had been with us in Birmingham constantly since Cayle's incident and, although hesitant to leave us, we encouraged him to spend some much-needed time with his family.

Cayle was stable and doing as well as could be expected. He had been on the oscillator for more than five days now and the combination of the 'God Machine' and him being rolled every two hours was working in loosening the mucus in his chest. The rolling was also taking the pressure off his sores. More X-rays revealed that there had been a slight improvement in his lung function over the past few days.

When I saw him that morning, my heart leapt with joy. He was spotlessly clean as the duty nurse had taken time to properly wash him down, shave his face and even brush his hair and his teeth. Although he would not be aware of it, it must have felt better. I asked her about the thin pieces of 'cotton' now visible between his lips and she explained, 'Those are the dissolving stitches used by the maxillofacial surgeon when the work was done on his mouth to start forming his lips.'

It had been more than a month since the incident and most of the bruising to his body had faded, leaving a slight yellowish tinge in some areas, particularly his top jawbone. The duty nurse had bandaged foam strips to Cayle's elbows because the action of the oscillator was constantly rubbing them against the bed sheet. His arms and abdomen were very swollen due to his body holding fluids as a consequence of the trauma. A diuretic was being administered.

* * *

Having already extended their trip once, it was now time for Janice and Michelle to leave us and they were flying back to Cape Town that night. VO John had come down from camp for his weekly visit, and to later drive the girls down to Heathrow Airport. They had hoped to be able to communicate with Cayle before they left but it wasn't to be. Work commitments were calling, plus Michelle had a family back home who needed her. There were tearful goodbyes to Cayle, each of them hugging him as gently as they could and in turn kissing his forehead. John stood by the bedside and told Cayle how proud he was of him.

Walking with them out to John's car, I couldn't thank the girls enough for their support. They had helped me through some very tough days and been a distraction in the nicest ways when I needed it. We'd walked for miles along the canals near the hospital, we'd chatted late into some nights, and we'd become more connected than ever. I was going to miss them terribly.

The following morning when I went to see Cayle, I met LC Andy Johnston at his bedside.

Dr Johnston (Consultant in Respiratory and Critical Care Medicine) was the consultant on duty. GC Ian Sargeant came by, stopping for an update. Together they made the decision to take a look at all of Cayle's wounds. It was the first time they were okay to leave me 'behind the curtain' with them while they did so. Chatting to Andy, Ian began to remove the dressing from Cayle's left hand. I started to back away. Noticing my movement, Ian asked, 'Have you seen the damage to Cayle's hand yet?'

'No,' I responded, feeling a little queasy, 'but I'm not sure I'm ready for that.'

I really do not know why Cayle's hand had worried me more than any of his other injuries – perhaps it was because I had always admired how masculine and strong they were. I also had a sense that it might bother him more than the loss of his legs would.

With what sounded like annoyance in his voice at my hesitation, Ian said, 'You'll have to see it sometime, so it's best you stay here now while I can explain what we have done – we've made huge progress.'

I took a very big breath and moved closer. Ian showed me how well the skin graft had taken on Cayle's palm and how the wounds on his fingers had closed. It was very evident from the expression on Ian's face that he was exceptionally pleased with the healing and Cayle's recovery overall. In fact, his exact words were, 'I don't see him falling at the last hurdle.'

Ian had remained positive throughout, and although Cayle's chances were still 50/50, he said he was erring on the positive side of 50. It felt as though a shaft of light had shone down and a weight was being ever so slightly lifted. I dared not get too excited, but I was so relieved that he had encouraged me to stay.

Later that afternoon when I popped in to say 'hi' to Cayle, I stood listening to the gentle chuff-chuffing of the oscillator. It reminded me of a steam train and I wondered if he would have any memory of it.

11. Dawn

Bronwyn
4 June 2012
Day 34

I was feeling excited yet apprehensive at the same time. It was 4 June and I had been awake for a lot of the night. Instead of the predicted three days, Cayle had been on the oscillator for six. This would be the day that he would be transferred from the oscillator back onto the conventional ventilator, but I could not fathom how it would be done. After all I had witnessed during the previous weeks, I should not have been surprised when the transfer worked precisely to plan.

Walking into ITU, it was comforting seeing the oscillator standing silently to one side, its duty completed, and the ventilator registering Cayle's steady breathing. Dr Johnston explained that all had gone smoothly and that Cayle's sedation had been dropped; as it wore off, he should start to open his eyes and move around.

Amazed but not surprised, Dr Johnston mentioned that when the switch-over was being done, Cayle seemed to be aware of what was happening. As I approached his bedside, Cayle slowly opened his eyes and looked at me. I had no idea how much he could see or even register through the haze of the combination of drugs and the eye ointments, but it was so good to see his eyes open again. I held his right hand with both of my hands.

'Hi,' I said.

He frowned a few times, and then squeezed my hands harder than I expected him to. I gasped and grinned. We shed a few tears, mine from the delight of seeing my son open his eyes and interact again; his, I think, for very different reasons, although I will never know what.

Making the most of the opportunity, I passed on a few messages of encouragement from various people and I was able to tell Cayle how much he is loved. I kissed his forehead numerous times saying, 'This is from ...., and this is from ...., and this is from ....', and I was sure he'd smiled.

I chatted away with him for some time but he got tired easily. It was time to leave him in the nurse's care.

<u>Patient diary entry, 2 am</u>

Hi Cayle. This is the third night on the trot that you've had to put up with me but at last we're letting you wake up and you're trying to go faster and quicker than we want – why am I not surprised!! Sister Hazel Lane

A few days followed where there was little change and Cayle seemed to go from being receptive to us to not wanting to engage at all. One morning, we were seated in FOB Royce catching up on admin when my phone lit up with 'DCCN' emblazoned across the screen.

I must admit that my heart sank a little ... no, that's a massive lie ... my heart sank a lot! 'Oh please, not again,' I thought. In fact, Claire was phoning to let me know that Cayle was very alert and that when she'd asked him if he wanted to see his mom, he had nodded.

I whooped so loudly that I startled a few people in the restaurant. Leaving the others behind, I hopped and skipped my way down the corridor to ITU, not in the least bit concerned about what anyone might think of me. It was worth it because I was not disappointed when I saw him.

The top half of the bed had been raised and he was in a semi-sitting position. From the look in his eyes it seemed he recognised me, although I had no way of knowing if he actually did. He seemed particularly unsettled though, appearing to swing from peace to anxiety fairly regularly. Just the sound of the cleaner's mop being knocked against the metal frame of a bed made him jump. He frowned often as he gazed around the ward seemingly thoroughly scrutinising everything.

Having been sedated for so many weeks, Cayle was finding it hard to coordinate his limbs, but it seemed that he very definitely wanted to feel his left hand with his right one. Richard was with us by then and he helped lift Cayle's right arm across for him to do so. I was unable to read his response and Cayle was unable to communicate with us, but I felt a sadness enveloping him.

He appeared to be getting more and more anxious. The nurse gently asked us to say goodnight so that she could clean him up and settle him for the night. I kissed his forehead and walked away with such heaviness in my heart for him. I hoped that a good night's sleep would ease his anxiety.

On our walk to the ward the following morning, I dared to let myself get excited. I hoped that as the drugs were eliminated from his system, Cayle would be less anxious and more responsive to us. I bobbed down the corridor alongside Seth, who was taking massive strides next to me.

'Mom!' Seth said with a laugh. 'What are you doing? Anyone would think that you're excited.'

By then we were both laughing. I knew that Cayle would be alert and that as the day went on he would become more aware of us and his surroundings. What I didn't expect was for it to happen quite so rapidly. He seemed delighted to see us and even tried to talk. I had to explain that for the time being he wouldn't be able to speak because he had a tracheostomy, but that soon it would be removed. He seemed unsure of what it meant but even so, he was slightly calmer than the previous day, although he tired quickly.

Going back in to say goodnight to him that evening was totally different. He smiled as soon as I saw him and he even winked, which made my heart leap.

'I want to kiss your forehead,' I said, 'but I can't reach you because I'm too short!'

I took hold of his right hand as he shuffled across towards me and lifted his head. He squeezed my hand. 'I love you, my child,' I said, and he smiled again and closed his eyes while I kissed his cheek. 'I have missed you more than you will ever know,' I said between sobs and giggles.

'Excuse me,' the nurse interrupted, 'but it's late and I need to settle him for the night.'

I was sorry to leave him.

'Goodnight. See you on the morrow.' It was a silly saying he and I often used and I smiled at having the chance to say it again.

As I walked away, one of the nurses came after me: 'Are your boys very close?'

'Yes,' I responded, 'very, very close. Why do you ask?'

'The smile on Cayle's face when he saw Seth walk into the ward this afternoon was absolutely priceless. He literally beamed. Unfortunately he probably won't remember it though.'

It continued to niggle me when it was constantly mentioned that Cayle would probably have no recollection of any of it – I wondered if it could still be true? He had seemed so aware of us. I took the opportunity to ask her, 'That is something we are told so often. Why do you think he won't remember?'

She replied, 'With the amount of sedation and medication he has been given, he is in a place between semi- and full consciousness. He is starting to recognise certain things, like his family, but his short-term memory will be fuzzy. He probably won't quite be able to discern the difference between dreams, hallucinations and reality. It will take time before he has total clarity.'

Then adding with a smile, 'His recovery has been phenomenal and nothing short of a miracle. All of us are keen to speak to him when that moment comes – he has become the talk of the ward.'

I proudly strutted out of ITU feeling like my heart was going to burst right out of my chest. I knew that when the time came, he would not disappoint.

* * *

As the days went by, it was fantastic to see the open spaces appearing beside his bed where the racks of drugs had been lined up for weeks.

Then one morning we got in to find Cayle subdued, staring at nothing. The relentless see-saw of highs and lows continued. He had not slept the previous night and he looked completely drained. Every few minutes his body started shaking uncontrollably. It was suggested that it was a result of all the intravenous medication having been switched off, which was giving him extreme withdrawal symptoms. He seemed overly anxious, although thankfully he had not tried to get off the bed again, something he constantly attempted.

When asked, he didn't remember anything from our time with him over the previous few days. My heart sank. However, when asked if he knew why he was in hospital, he did remember the incident. We assumed he was having flash-backs, which would account for his extreme anxiety.

I stood at the bedside and stroked his forehead, willing him to sleep. Eventually his eyes would close, but a moment later they would spring open again. It was very distressing to watch; I could not even begin to imagine what he was going through.

Before leaving the hospital that evening, I asked if Cayle would be given something to help him sleep, only to be told that he would be left without medication for as long as possible as his body needed to find its own routine. I understood the logic but it did not seem likely that sleep was going to come any time soon.

* * *

After the Spring Bank Holiday weekend, I happened to be at Cayle's bedside during military doctors' rounds. I was delighted to see the various consultants' reactions regarding how much he had improved. Many of them had not seen him since he had been connected to the oscillator with only a 50/50 chance of survival. They marvelled at the speed at which his body was healing externally, but the condition of his chest was of most interest. Results from a chest X-ray were in and Ian Sargeant gave instructions for Cayle to be taken off the ventilator for a few hours at a time and just an oxygen mask be placed over the tracheostomy hole. Cayle's oxygen levels were constantly monitored in case they fell, but he coped well. This was a huge boost for me – soon the tracheostomy would be removed and finally we would be able to hear Cayle speak again.

Spending time with Seth at Cayle's bedside later that day, he started making a few jokes with Cayle and we could see the corners of his eyes crinkle up. Slowly we were beginning to catch little glimpses of the Cayle we knew. The combination of this new breathing technique, however, and the general lack of sleep meant that he tired quickly and so we said an early goodnight to him.

Two steps forwards, one step back; three steps forward, two steps back; five steps forward, one step back. We had heard this since the day Cayle was admitted to QEHB. Walking into ITU to be told by the DCCN, 'He's still not sleeping, despite being given sleeping medication', felt like it was a couple of steps back.

How could it possibly be? I was shocked to learn that he had slept for less than an hour. This meant that he had had less than two hours of sleep in more than seventy-two hours. He looked truly exhausted. He wouldn't even look at us, let alone engage in any other way. I was desperate to help him, to know what was going on inside his head. We'd been doing everything we were told to, reassuring him constantly that he was safe, that he was back in the UK with us. We just weren't sure how much he had processed. I'd wondered – if the tracheostomy had been removed, would he be speaking to us?

Richard and I walked over to his bedside and, although wide-eyed, he didn't respond. He followed me with his eyes but he never reacted when I asked him to nod or blink.

I went in search of GC Ian Sargeant, who told me, 'I went to chat to Cayle earlier this morning to introduce myself. He does seem very anxious. I told him that he has a lot to come to terms with and to adjust to. I'm honestly not sure how I would cope in Cayle's situation, but one thing I do know is that Cayle is a stronger man than me. I've no idea how much he took in but I hope he understood me.'

Cayle had proved against all odds that he was a fighter and now was not the time to give up.

Later in the day, Dr Johnston came to FOB Royce to find Richard and me.

'Cayle's heart rate suddenly went from 110 to 170+,' he said. 'I've administered something to calm him down. The sedatives he has been on can cause terrible side effects, one of them being hallucinations. The morphine will probably already be out of his system by now, but the other sedatives could take up to two weeks to flush through.'

It would be a matter of time.

Cayle had been blessed with an iPad with a note attached reading 'You are a hero'. It had been kindly donated to him by the children of Jimi Heselden, the wealthy entrepreneur who founded Hesco Bastion in 1989. The company manufactured containers of the same name: when filled with sand or earth, they allowed effective blast walls and barriers to be quickly constructed and they were used by the armies of several countries. Mr Heselden had made a large donation to Help for Heroes a few years before his tragic death in 2010. Receiving this unexpected gift greatly touched us; it came with a realisation that there are people who do not even know Cayle and yet they still consider him a hero.

Seth loaded the iPad with a music playlist and a few films and when I went to say goodnight that evening, Cayle was still wide awake and staring, but the music was playing through the earphones and thankfully he seemed a little calmer.

* * *

Two days later, the duty consultant, who had been on leave for a week, stopped by to speak to us. 'I am truly amazed at the speed of Cayle's recovery. He has come so far in just one week. I have given instructions for syringes of water to be squirted into his mouth to check his swallow reflex. If he copes, liquid and solid foods will slowly be introduced orally, starting with ice cream.'

This raised a wry smile and I thanked him. Cayle has never had a sweet tooth but he does have a weakness for ice cream. This was all beginning to sound very positive and I felt as though I could finally breathe just a little easier.

Cayle

I remember massive discomfort; pain in the back of my head, pain in my lower back, everything ached. There was a basin about a metre away from my bed. I was looking at it thinking I just wanted to get water, I need water. I was absolutely boiling hot and my tongue was so dry. I couldn't talk and I couldn't do anything, so I couldn't even ask to have a sip or anything. It was torture. I just wanted to stick my head under the cold tap and let it pour over me. That was horrible – I absolutely hated it. I was too weak to move and I was in so much pain. I was uncomfortable but too weak to roll myself over. I was just getting propped up by nurses and listening to the beeps and bleeps of machines and the cries of discomfort of other patients. No matter how hard I tried I could not sleep. It was awful.

On our way out of QEHB that evening, we saw GC Sargeant. 'I will be more disappointed than ever if Cayle doesn't make it. I now believe that he has a 95 per cent chance of survival.'

What incredible news to hear from Ian after all that time. I was elated and hoped that it would be for real. But would it? It had been a long and bumpy road, filled with potholes and pebbles. Every time I had dared to believe that Cayle was fine, another hazard had appeared.

'No,' I reprimanded myself for my doubt, 'I choose to believe that he is going to be fine.'

Finally it seemed that a solution had been found for getting Cayle to sleep. A television had been brought to his bedside and when we popped in to say good morning, he was fast asleep with a football match showing. What a chuckle we had – Cayle has always hated football.

With the drone of the television in the background, he slept most of the day away. We could not have been happier.

12. Rebirth

Bronwyn
17 June 2012
Day 48

The day started slowly, with Cayle initially being unresponsive.

Richard and I went to see him at about noon. His bed-space was being packed up because he was about to be moved away from the dark area directly in front of the nurses' station, a space reserved for *critical* critical patients.

Making casual chat in the hopes of getting him to engage, I mentioned to Cayle all the letters he had received from his army mates. 'Now that you are awake, I can start reading them to you.'

He raised his eyebrows and I knew I had his attention. His eyes were alive again and it was incredible to witness.

Before I could go any further, a group of nurses and assistants appeared and surrounded the bed. I joined the procession as Cayle was wheeled round the corner to a space closer to a window. Once he had been settled, the ventilator switched off and an oxygen mask once again placed over his tracheostomy, I told him, 'You've been moved from the dark side to the light.' He smiled with his mouth and with his eyes as I continued, 'And you must be loving having all the girls running around you!'

In typically Cayle style, he had wiggled his eyebrows. I longed to give him a huge bear-hug but settled for kissing him on the forehead, not easily achieved when, with a cheeky look in his eyes, he'd moved his head away as I leaned forward. He started to chuckle and I am not sure if it was him or me who had been more surprised.

Out of the pocket of his body warmer, which I had continued to wear, I took a couple of carefully selected letters. Starting slowly,

I read to him news from 'his' boys. He listened intently, but by the time I was nearing the end of the second letter, I could see that he was tiring. I carefully refolded it and placed it back in the pocket and when I looked up, he had nodded off.

I stood staring at him for some time as he slept, his eyelids constantly moving. What was going through his subconscious, I wondered. As the weeks had gone by, his powerful body had literally shrunk before our eyes. He had seemed as weak as a newborn, barely able to lift his head. So much external healing had now taken place. It had been fascinating to watch the miracle of his body, almost completely destroyed, being stapled and sewn back together, and then nature taking over. Those who had seen him periodically over the previous weeks had remarked on his extraordinary recovery. Being with him every single day had enabled us to watch his body being restored, but it was an additional comfort to hear from others how dramatic the healing had been and how perfectly his skin had knitted together in such a short time. Clean scars remained as visible evidence of the physical hurt. However, it was the invisible scars that were starting to concern me more.

When I went to say goodnight to him that evening, the nurse told me that she had been busy with the patient in the bed next to Cayle's when out of the corner of her eye she saw Cayle sitting upright on his bed. We were not to be fooled by his apparent weakness.

The very next day I walked into ITU to see Ian Sargeant holding Cayle's hand and the two of them laughing together. It was the most thrilling sight for me. I was sure that my broad grin conveyed it, but it was nothing in comparison to the smile on Cayle's face.

Ian was telling him, 'You need to start stretching your arms above your head, across your chest, scratch your nose, touch your ear – anything to get your strength back.'

As doggedly determined as he has ever been and with intense concentration, Cayle immediately started to lift his now-slender arms. The sheer effort of it was apparent on his face. He had dropped from

86 kg down to 59 kg, and although a large portion of that was due to the loss of his legs, he had lost a lot of weight and muscle too.

Ian turned to me, 'I think he's back!'

I laughed and cried at the same time. For forty-eight long days, Cayle had stared death in the face and he'd defied the odds.

'Hi,' I choked. He smiled while continuing to move his arms about.

'Cayle is being fed 6,000 calories a day through his feeding tube. Bearing in mind that the average man should consume 2,500 calories a day, this should bode well for his recovery.'

'I'll leave you two alone now,' said Ian as he moved to walk away, adding: 'He has a lot to come to terms with. Try not to overwhelm him with too much information too soon.'

I stood beside Cayle's bed and he shakily reached out for my hand. In that instant I knew that my son was finally back from the dark world he had lived in for the past forty-eight days. I so wanted to embrace him and, as I held onto his slim right hand, I could see that his whole countenance had changed. His eyes searched mine, desperately wanting answers. I hesitated, unsure of how much he remembered … from the incident, from his time in hospital, from our chats – how would I know where to start?

Ian's words sprung to mind and I was mindful not to bombard Cayle.

I chatted away excitedly, passing on some of the messages I had been given for him. He nodded in acknowledgement.

'It didn't take us long to work out that some people are hand holders and others are head strokers,' I told him, and we both chuckled.

'We have a lot to catch up on,' I continued, 'but first you need to eat something. Nurse Sarah is going to do the honours.'

We'd all laughed.

I stood by as Sarah attempted to get some ice cream into Cayle's mouth, the first solid food he'd had in almost seven weeks. A combination of the neck brace and a mouth that had been reformed by surgery meant that Cayle was only able to part his lips a few millimetres. This resulted in ice cream dripping all down his chin and into his neck brace, but what little did go in must have seemed like an explosion of flavour in his mouth. Sarah made the most of the situation by asking him to lick his lips or roll his tongue around his mouth, all forms of encouraging muscle use in and around his mouth area.

Through my mind flashed an image of Cayle at about 10 months old. I'd come home from the grocery store to find him standing holding onto the front gate with a huge grin on his face. Out of the corner of his mouth was dangling just the tail of a gecko lizard. The rest he must have already eaten.

Padre Jonathon had heard that Cayle was alert, so he stopped by to chat.

'Hello, Cayle – so nice to meet you properly at last! I'm Jonathon the padre and I've been waiting to take you downstairs to Costa for a coffee.'

I left the two of them to get acquainted and went in search of Richard and Seth.

As I was leaving the ward I saw Ian. We walked out into the corridor together and I began, 'Ian, thank you for saving Cayle's life.'

He tried to play it down. 'Don't thank me – it has been a team effort.'

'I realise that,' I said, 'but you are an integral part of that team.'

'He came within a hair's breadth of dying,' he said as he gave me a hug; we walked in the direction of FOB Royce with an arm around each other.

'I am quite sure I am as pleased about Cayle's recovery as you are. You have every right to be exceptionally proud of your son.'

Leaving the hospital that evening, we made a group decision to go straight to the pub for a celebratory drink or two. I wanted to shout from the rooftops that my son had survived and was well on the road to recovery. By the time the next day rolled around, however, our heads definitely didn't want to hear any shouting.

* * *

After forty-eight days in a coma, the following day was the first that Cayle was not running a high temperature, and what a blessing it was. At one stage he even attempted to pull the sheet up over his chest because he was so cool.

Seth asked to be alone with Cayle and he took with him a pile of letters from Cayle's army friends. According to the nurses, gales of laughter could be heard across the ward as the brothers shared precious time alone.

I waited at FOB Royce, doing some admin on my phone when the padre appeared.

'Cayle is obviously well on his way to recovery now,' he said with a huge smile on his face.

'Oh, have you been to see him already?' I asked.

'No, but I see you aren't wearing his jacket for the first time!'

I hadn't even realised, but subconsciously I was aware that Cayle had passed the critical stage and felt comfortable enough not to wear it. It was, however, tucked safely into my handbag next to me. The dog tags remained around my neck.

After quiet-time, I went to see Cayle.

'Another letter has arrived from one of your mates in Afghanistan – would you like me to read it to you?'

He shook his head and indicated that he wanted to actually see it. I held it up for him and watched his eyes scanning across the lines as he read it himself. The joy was twofold for me – it was the first real confirmation we'd had that he'd not lost the vision in his left eye, but also that he was able to concentrate enough to read and absorb what was written. I noticed that the bright lights in the ward bothered his very sensitive eyes though.

When we said goodnight that evening, Cayle seemed so much calmer and quite comfortable. As we walked away, he picked up his hand to wave to us. Seth turned back and went to hug him. The juxtaposition of Seth, an immensely fit Royal Marine, and Cayle, a mere shadow of his former self, was both heartrending and heart-warming at the same time. I could feel the immense love between them and a huge lump formed in my throat. My boys. That image is one I have imprinted in my memory.

It was absolutely fantastic to see the buzz that Cayle's recovery had caused on the ward. People who had worked with him were keen to meet him; a constant flow stopping by to introduce themselves and congratulate him on his astounding recovery. He was baffled by the attention, unaware of the trauma he had been through.

Cayle was yet to discover the full extent of his injuries.

We walked into ITU one morning just after doctors' rounds and could instantly tell that he was upset about something. Still unable to speak because of the tracheostomy, he used his iPad to write 'gutted didn't know I lost both legs'.

Cayle

When I got blown up I could kind of see what was going on still. I saw that my legs had been completely smashed – the right one was attached by a thread but it was still attached. When I woke up in hospital after the coma, I was too weak to sit up, so I was laid flat on my back. I had no idea what phantom pains were, so when I woke up and I could feel my right leg and I could wiggle my toes I thought, 'Oh, wow, this is brilliant, they've actually saved it – I've lost my left leg and I've got some dings and scars but I can work around that.' I didn't realise that the right leg had been amputated above the knee as well. Especially after two or three days of lying on my back and thinking, 'I've got a leg and it's not that bad.' I didn't realise how bad my left hand was. It was in bandages, but I didn't think that I was missing parts of all of my fingers, and I certainly didn't know what my face looked like. I'd never had Xboxes or that kind of stuff and I was thinking I could bring myself to play some Xbox in the meantime because I'm going to go absolutely mental just sitting around doing nothing. I could also work on my really terrible guitar-playing. It was only when they took the bandages off my left hand and I thought, 'Hey, why don't you just punch me in the testicles again.' They bring this thing out and I thought, 'Huh?' because everyone had said, 'You should see what they've done with your hand – it's amazing to see what they've managed to do.' Now, in my mind amazing would be having fingers and a moveable thumb. To be fair, when I saw the state of my hand, the real medical photos of it, it's stomach-churning. I don't really suffer seeing graphic stuff, but this was like – wow, they did an outstanding job of saving what they did. Still, in my mind I was painting this picture of I could still do this and this, but unfortunately this is what I ended up with, which was a devastating kick. So the guitar sits silent.

Although we had been telling him about his injuries over the previous weeks, the drugs prevented him from comprehending any of it. The emptiness in his eyes was like nothing I had ever seen from him. I couldn't tell from his expression what his exact thoughts were, but I hoped it wasn't that he wished he hadn't lived. I wished I could cocoon him from his new reality.

* * *

Over the next few days, things started to move quite quickly. Cayle was completely off the ventilator and an oxygen mask lay loosely over the tracheostomy. This enabled him to have much more freedom of movement.

'We are awaiting CT neck scan results and, all being well, we are hoping to hoist him into a sitting position for up to twenty minutes at a time, slowly building it up so that we can move him into a wheelchair,' Ian said.

An hour later, Cayle was sitting in a chair. Initially he motioned that he was feeling very light-headed. He had been prostrate for so long that his body had become unaccustomed to being upright. While he was sitting, he was gesturing something. We failed the guessing game, so he had to write on the iPad that he was sitting on the catheter tube, which was causing a bit of back-pressure. This caused much hilarity and was a sure way of knowing that Cayle still had his sense of humour.

* * *

Each day brought with it more positives, every one of them encouraging Cayle to keep going. My youngest sister, Anthea, over from South Africa, arrived on 21 June. I knew she would not only be of enormous emotional help to me, but to Cayle as well.

Nearing his bed, we could see his smile from across the ward.

'Hi,' he said as we got closer, 'my trachy has been removed.'

I literally whooped and burst into tears at the same time, clapping and jumping up and down on the spot, then instantly remembered that we were in ITU when I was shushed. With a speaking valve fitted to his tracheostomy, it was so exciting hearing Cayle actually say something after all that time and I realised with much relief that – although a bit gravelly – his voice sounded much the same. I was sure that this would make an enormous difference to his mental recovery.

It was clear when we chatted that Cayle remembered the whole incident very vividly and he was speaking about it openly with us all. We had numerous 'if only' discussions, but as he said, 'Nothing can change what has happened.'

I was humbled by the way he seemed to be dealing with it.

* * *

Our days now consisted of extreme highs and the lowest of lows. I was enormously grateful to have Anthea with me to share them. Arriving at the hospital and on our way to FOB Royce, we passed the DCCN.

'Cayle will be moving up to Ward 412 this morning,' he announced with glee.

Ward 412 is on the second floor of the hospital, the ward where soldiers were transferred to once considered stable enough to leave ITU.

Cayle's bed had been loaded up with the little equipment he would still need and we were on the move. It felt truly like a royal bypass as nurses and medical staff lined the corridors. There were whoops of joy and cheers, even a few tears. Many had commented that they were thrilled at his recovery but sorry to be saying goodbye. Even in adversity, he had made an impression. He promised that he would somehow get down to visit them all when he was fully mobilised in a wheelchair.

It was very apt that Dr Sinclair had been with us at the start of the journey and there she was standing to one side. Beaming, I went over to shake her hand but she pushed it aside and gave me a hug instead.

'Thank you for everything you have done,' I said. To which she responded, 'I'm delighted to have been a part of the success of Cayle's recovery, but none of the medical staff can take the credit – it is Cayle's fitness, incredibly strong heart and his will to survive that has pulled him through.'

* * *

We'd met Bryan Philips a few days earlier when he'd been admitted to ITU and he was in the bed alongside Cayle's. Bryan was also a double amputee as a result of his incident, but he'd not suffered the internal injuries that Cayle had. He'd had a couple of family members at his bedside and I couldn't help but notice, selfishly and with a twinge of jealousy, that he was having a laugh with them, while we had had so many weeks of uncertainty while Cayle's survival hung in the balance. I instantly felt guilty that the thought had even crossed my mind. Two days later Bryan was moved out of ITU to 412.

Up on 412 we were welcomed to what would be Cayle's new home for the foreseeable future. His bed was alongside a window and across from him in the four-bed ward was Bryan. We exchanged greetings with him.

Cayle

Lying in bed was miserable and I absolutely hated it, but the nurses did their best and they were always very smiley and warm. No matter what happened, they were there to help, and the surgeons and doctors were all brilliant. It's interesting having a military ward up on 412 because you're in a room with guys who have similar injuries or at least similar backgrounds and experiences. Having Bryan in the bed opposite helped a lot, although I couldn't sit myself up. I remember being massively jealous of the fact that he could just sit up in bed even though he had no legs. He had not been in a coma in ITU and was fortunately only in there for a few days, so he hadn't had the muscle wastage I had. I was hugely envious of the fact that he could sit there and watch films and hop in a wheelchair and buzz around the place and I couldn't even roll myself over or get myself back up the bed once I'd slid down. But we became good friends and had plenty of laughs.

Once settled in, Cayle had asked for a mirror. It was a moment I had been dreading and I was relieved that Richard and Seth were with us. Bright daylight streamed through the window and it was incredibly tough to watch my beautiful son stare at the reflection that stared back at him, empty eyed. He had woken to a world far removed from the familiar one he knew. We stood by, holding our breath, and with our hearts in our mouths. We could see how his face had knitted together again after all that time, but he could only see the scars and devastation caused by the explosion. It was heartbreaking to witness and Cayle never uttered a word, handing the mirror back to Seth.

Soon after, the physiotherapists came in to check on Cayle.

'How soon can I get out of this bed and into a wheelchair?' he asked. It was heartening that he was confronting his recovery with the same resolute determination he had applied to every other challenge he had ever faced. Within fifteen minutes a hoist was placed next to his bed and an electric wheelchair appeared. Three people had to assist with the lift because they needed to be careful of his broken neck, but they carefully placed him in the chair. The instructions given to him were that he must operate the wheelchair on speed one until he was used to it. With this newfound freedom, and in typical Cayle style, as soon as he was out of the ward and into the corridor, the speed was cranked up to two and he was on his way to the common room at the end of the corridor. The common room was equipped with sofas and a coffee machine, and quite often laden with cakes and other delicacies kindly donated by the public. It was to become the new FOB Royce during visiting times.

Safely back in his bed an hour later, he looked exhausted. He had not slept for the previous few nights. Now away from the beeps and buzzes that accompanied ITU, I said, 'Hopefully 412 will be much quieter and you will be able to get some sleep tonight.'

'I've been asleep since the second of May,' he quipped, 'and now that I am finally awake, all you guys are doing is trying to make me sleep again.' We'd all laughed.

There it was again – the sense of humour that I honestly believed would be a major factor in helping him through his rehabilitation. Interspersed between the heavy times, Cayle was entertaining us with his comments. From a Ben and Jerry's ice cream feast, in which we all partook, and he aptly named a 'diabetic's nightmare', to telling us that he should take up kayaking because he could use his left hand as a paddle, he was able to get us laughing.

* * *

Although in constant contact with me since Cayle's incident, Brigadier Chris Dick had refrained from visiting until an opportune time. Once Cayle was out of ITU and able to converse, I invited Chris to come up to QEHB. The timing was perfect because Cayle was more mobile by then and he was able to get himself down to the common room. Chris took the time to explain to him just a few of the opportunities available once he had completed his rehabilitation. He reiterated that Cayle would receive all the support he needed from him, and any other support that Chris could muster. It gave us a chance to air our concerns, mostly regarding accommodation once Cayle returned to Dartmouth as he would not be able to access my flat. It was very comforting to know that amid all that was going on, we didn't have to worry about anything, even the most trivial things. This meeting was very important for all of us.

Our afternoon visit was totally different from the seriousness of the session that morning. When Cayle was first admitted to QEHB he was given such a slim chance of survival that, when it came to stitching his face together and creating new lips for him, it didn't seem the most important thing that the surgeons had left a small gap around the left side of his mouth where there wasn't enough flesh to bring the lips together. Cayle began telling us that he had just used mouthwash for the first time.

'So I filled my mouth up and began sloshing it around but it just squirted out of the side and onto my chest!' he said indignantly.

He had also begun sending through food requests – grapes one day and Jelly Babies the next. Some of the requests seemed rather random until we worked out that it seemed to be that whatever Bryan was eating, Cayle suddenly had a craving for. We were more than happy to oblige. His appetite was definitely increasing, the very physically intense physiotherapy being the major contributing factor.

The following afternoon the ward consultant stopped by to ask Cayle if he had any questions about anything. He took the opportunity to ask her if it would be possible for him to see his X-rays and CT scans, right from Role 3 in Afghanistan up to him being in Critical B. She immediately went to fetch the COW (Computer on Wheels) on which the hospital's database could be accessed and she pulled up Cayle's file. He was able to select whichever X-rays he wanted to view first and he chose to look at his left hand. It had far more metal in it than any of us had realised and she called it his bionic hand. Next was his lungs; she showed us the X-ray from Camp Bastion and then the image taken around the time he was put onto the oscillator when his lungs were completely whited out. I think that was when Cayle finally started to catch a tiny glimpse of how far he had come.

After the consultant left the bedside, we decided to have a cherry celebration. There was a fruit vendor outside the hospital entrance that sold a variety of deliciously fresh fruits and every day Cayle would put in his request. That day it was for cherries. It was good exercise for Cayle because he had to stretch his mouth wide enough to fit them in. I would push a cherry into his mouth, he would chew the flesh off the stone and then pop the stone out of his mouth and we tried to catch them. Unfortunately the bed sheets came off worse as the slippery stones were quite difficult to hold on to, resulting in burgundy stains all over the covers. We were all suitably cherried out afterwards and so was his bed, but the antics had given us all some light relief.

A little later, a nurse appeared to inspect Bryan's dressings. As she was pulling the curtains around his bed she looked across and saw Cayle. Her face lit up and she walked over to him.

'Hi … it's great to see you again!' she enthused.

Having no idea who she was, Cayle was taken by surprise until she went on, 'I was onboard the C-17 that brought you back from Afghanistan. I heard about your miraculous recovery but I am so pleased to see you with my own eyes. I must admit that we didn't hold out much hope for your survival, so it's fantastic to see you.'

They exchanged a few words and then we had the opportunity to thank her for the role she had played in saving his life.

* * *

Almost nine weeks after injury, we took the first photograph of Cayle. He was lying on his bed and wearing Seth's sunglasses because his eyes were still so sensitive to the light. He bravely gave a thumbs-up to Seth, who snapped the shot. It was a reminder to us of how much his head had swelled up after injury. Now, with a combination of the massive reduction in weight plus his body no longer retaining excess fluids, he seemed lost in the huge neck brace that appeared to engulf him.

Visiting hours on Ward 412 were stricter than in ITU, but sometimes I was able to spend time alone with Cayle. I'd asked the physiotherapists if there was anything I could assist with and had been told that massaging his scars would help prevent them tethering to the underlying muscles. When visiting hours were over, I'd take out the ointment and start massaging his scars. I was then allowed to remain by his bedside for longer.

We had many very deep and emotional conversations during those times. In one of them, Cayle asked me to hand him a mirror so that he could inspect his face.

'Maybe one day I'll come to accept losing my legs. I suppose I can hide my left hand in my pocket, but I'll never be able to get away from the stares of people when they see my face.'

What was I supposed to say to that? Words escaped me. I knew that Cayle had always hoped to achieve some amazing things in his life and he looked at me with such despair in his eyes. 'Mom, what am I going to do now?'

My heart literally ached for him.

'Cayle, I have no idea how, but doors are going to open for you that would never have opened before.'

I was trusting that he would soon begin to realise how much he'd still be capable of. At 26, he had a full life ahead of him and I knew that he would go on to do great things. I was able to tell him about the hundreds of people around the world who had been praying for his survival and recovery, and his response was, 'How am I ever going to thank them?'

During another of our extended chats, he wanted to know every detail of how I had been told about his incident. He went on to ask questions about our time at QEHB while he was in his coma. I'd tried to describe the ebb and flow of emotions as simply as I could without wanting to overload him. Hoping to give him a glimpse of how much we had all struggled, I said, 'Cayle, I'm so relieved that you don't have a girlfriend because it would have meant emotionally supporting someone else through this and it's been hard enough with just us.'

His expression had instantly changed and I saw a mixture of anger and defeat,

'Well what are my chances now? Who is going to want to be with me like this?'

Instantly I regretted speaking my mind.

Richard would also spend copious amounts of time chatting to Cayle. In fact he was far better at it than I was. I found that I started crying way too often and I knew that I wasn't always who he needed. I was desperate to say the right things but I'd never felt so helpless.

'Mom, it's not good for you or for me if you sit here and cry all the time,' he gently said. 'There's nothing we can do now about what has happened. If you can't sit here without constantly crying, it would be better if you left me alone.'

When he'd been in a coma and unaware of the damage done, I'd felt slightly more able to handle things. As soon as he was awake and having to process and accept the cards he'd been dealt, I seemed to be far less able to control my emotions, knowing that he had so many challenges ahead. The physical pain in his body was no longer anaesthetised by the cocktail of drugs he had been on, and he had to face the harsh reality of what this horrific incident had left him with.

It seemed the complete opposite for Richard, who was far more at peace now that Cayle was out of the coma, stable, and that they could communicate. The enormous sense of helplessness that Richard had felt which caused his outbursts in those first weeks seemed to have lessened. He had been able to encourage Cayle with new opportunities that he may have. They even discussed the latest prosthetic legs and technology that Richard had done some Internet research on.

One particular evening remains etched in my mind. I entered the ward to find Cayle staring, eyes completely glazed over.

'Hi,' I said.

He remained quiet for a few moments and then, tilting his head ever so slightly on the pillow, he looked at me with incredible sadness in his eyes.

'Mom, why didn't you give permission to switch the machines off?'

Of all the things he could have asked, I had not expected that. I grappled for words while doing my utmost to contain my emotions.

'Cayle, never once was I asked. Your body fought the whole time. Your heart remained incredibly strong – we could feel it beating through the steel frame when we leaned against your bed. Even when you were sedated and on various breathing machines, your instinct was to breathe for yourself. Your body's will to survive surpassed everyone's expectations. You have to remember that you can't get through a war without scars; yours will just be more visible than most others.'

Years later I learned from Cayle that the reason he had asked me was not because he had wanted to die but because he was feeling guilty about what we were going through as a result of his incident. He felt it would have been better if he had not survived. When I heard this, I was saddened to my core.

13. Hell

Cayle

While I was in a coma I had no concept of time. I didn't really know what was going on. I was just in this weird state of hallucinating between seemingly endless dreams. There were a number of bizarre ones, most of them being particularly dark and grim, terrifying and horrible. A lot of the time that I lay there my eyes were open and I seemed awake, taking in what was around me but so heavily sedated that my mind was warping everything.

In one particular dream I was lying in the hospital bed, completely paralysed but totally awake and conscious. I could see and hear everything that was going on, but the doctors thought that I was dead. I was trying to scream that I was alive. I wasn't dead but I couldn't move, I couldn't blink, I couldn't do anything. Because I was wounded but my torso was in good order, they decided to use me for organ donation. They brought out these horrific-looking steel surgical tools and they started to disembowel me, removing one organ at a time. I could see them placing the organs in iced containers next to the bed, the blood pouring down their arms as they moved them over. For some reason I wasn't dying. I was still alive and once they were done they took a scalpel to my eyes and cut a pair of deep crosses into them to show that I had been harvested. Now that I had been picked clean of anything useful to them they were going to send me upstairs to the crematorium. There was an elevator just in front of my bed that they were putting people into and sending them up. I was trying to scream and shout to tell them that I was still alive, but they put me into this upright elevator and sent me up to the crematorium where I was pushed into an oven and burnt. I felt a flash of heat and then there was nothing but darkness. As it turns out, when I finally came out of my coma weeks later, I could see what the 'elevator' was – it was the large ceiling-mounted power block that was above the bed, the unit that all of my life support was powered from. It was this big chunky thing hanging from the ceiling with a clock on it. It was quite weird to see it and realise what it was post-waking up.

* * *

Another one was when I was lying in my bed and again unable to move, but I could talk. One of the people who was walking around the hospital looked a bit shifty and suspicious. He decided to grab my bed and run me out of the hospital. He stuck me in the back of a van and kidnapped me. He drove off and I didn't know where we were going or what was happening. Eventually he needed to stop but he didn't want to leave me behind in case I somehow escaped or was found. So he wheeled me in my hospital bed into a coffee shop for a quick stop. I mentioned to him that the route he was taking me on meant that we would be going past the source of the Amazon River and I thought it would be worth stopping. He didn't want to go and I was furious – I was so angry that the guy who had kidnapped me wasn't going to allow me to go and see the source of the Amazon River. We continued down the motorway until we got to a warehouse. He unloaded me into a dark, dingy room and tied me down in a weird position. He then set up an overhead camera and started taking photographs, changing my position each time. I watched as he uploaded the images onto his computer and started to manipulate them. Suddenly I realised what he was doing – he was trying to make me look like Prince Harry. Clearly he wanted to make it appear as if he had captured the prince so he could collect a huge ransom. I was telling him that no one was ever going to believe him, that I look nothing like Prince Harry. But he wouldn't listen. When I woke up from my coma I discovered that the bloke who had 'kidnapped' me was actually one of the friendliest nurses there.

* * *

I can remember one period that was quite grim where Mom and Dad were sitting by my bed and I was trying to warn them of the dangers of where they were. We were sitting in a hospital in the middle of nowhere, deep in Afghanistan. I could not work out how they had even managed to get there. There was this weird, gloomy green/yellow light to the whole place and, all around, angry faces with piercing eyes but no obvious facial features stared intensely at me. I still had my pistol with me and I was clutching it tightly to my chest with my right hand and holding a spare magazine in my left. I remember not being able to sleep at all because I was so worried that something was going to happen to my folks. I lay awake ready to do battle with anybody who came in. I was lying in a hospital bed, so I already knew that I was injured, although I had no recollection as to how I had ended up in the hospital, only that I had been in an incident while out on an operation and now that they were both there, I could not let anything happen to them. I wasn't ready to die and I certainly wasn't going to let my folks be injured as well. I just couldn't rest. Mom and Dad were saying, 'You've got to sleep, you've got to let go of the pistol, you've got to sleep, you've got to sleep.' They were telling me that it was going to be okay but I just couldn't sleep. After the coma I remember finding out that I hadn't slept for days. It must have been that particular point when I was so anxious that somebody was going to die that I just couldn't sleep.

* * *

I had been injured and I was lying propped up against a wall in a tiny hut on a rattan mat on the floor. I think it was high in the mountains in Nepal or somewhere like that. I was screaming for a nurse or a doctor because my legs were amputated and I was bleeding out on the floor. As much as I screamed, nobody was coming. I remember a random goat walking around in this hut; it raised its head and looked at me and then carried on about its business. This was apparently a hospital but nobody ever turned up. I was sinking lower and lower down the wall as the blood was running out of me. I knew I was dying. I could feel the life slowly draining out of me. I looked out the door of the hut at the mountain view and saw my indifferent goat companion grazing happily away as everything faded to black.

* * *

Don't read Dante and then get blown up in Afghan. I found myself falling through the different circles of hell unaccompanied by a Virgil of my own. I kept dying in each circle after experiencing its terrifying sounds, smells, horrors and pains before progressing to the next. With each death I knew I was one step closer to finding myself before the Devil himself, deep down in the dark depths. As I fell lower and lower and further down I just remember thinking, 'How am I dying again? I am not ready for this. What have I done to deserve this?' And yet I would still die and progress to the deeper and darker realms of hell. The overwhelming sense of insignificance and an inability to stop the horrific descent into the depths was truly terrifying. I never did find myself in front of the Devil. Instead it was just me in an endless blackness, this dark, freezing, all-consuming nothingness. Abandon all hope indeed.

* * *

In another, I was sitting on a mat on a dusty wooden floor. The room had a low ceiling and a staircase that led up to a dark room above. There was a strange dull yellow glow downstairs. I still had my arms and my legs and I was there with Mom and Dad and Seth. They did not belong there and were simply waiting to see my judgement. There were other faceless people sitting in groups in the room and I could see them talking but I couldn't hear the words. They seemed to be waiting for something, although I could not tell what. Suddenly there was a bellowing roar and the sound of heavy, hoof-like footsteps on the wooden floor above. The footsteps moved slowly from left to right across the floor above and an enormous figure emerged from the shadows at the top of the stairs. It was a minotaur – it had the legs of a bull, a muscular human torso, and the head of an ox. I could hear its breathing, deep and loud. It came down the stairs and when it reached the bottom, I could see that everyone else in the room had put their thumbs flat on the floor as if in submission. Mom looked at me, urging me with her eyes to do the same, but I was unsure as to how I should respond. The beast turned to me and I could feel its anger. It bellowed and strode across the room and began beating me. I could feel its knuckles crunching into my bone and its hooves kicking me. The groups around the room did not even lift their heads, their eyes and thumbs fixed to the floor, helpless and terrified. Finally the beating stopped and the beast turned and walked back up the stairs. It seemed like hours passed and I could hear people talking but I couldn't hear what they were saying. And then I heard the same awful roar and the footsteps on the wooden boards and I knew that the creature was coming back. This time I copied everyone and put my thumbs on the ground, pressing down hard. It chose someone else to beat and I heard the thud of beaten flesh and crunching bone. And so it went on. It seemed like weeks or even months and none of us moved on but the beast kept coming back. It never spoke; it only interacted with violence. The minotaur wanted submission and we were its prisoners.

* * *

I think it was the day after I started to come out of my coma and I still didn't understand that I had a tracheostomy. Actually, I didn't know what was going on at all. Seth was standing next to the bed during a visit and it must have been another hallucination, or maybe at that point it was just a dream. I was telling him how I had climbed up Mount Kenya the day before and I had base-jumped off of it in a wing-suit. I had flown in this wing-suit off Mount Kenya successfully and landed down below. I was telling Seth, 'Don't worry, dude, everything is going to be okay. Can you believe I base-jumped off Mt Kenya yesterday. Don't worry about me, I'm going to be fine!'

Later that night as my mind started to become more and more clear of the drugs, I realised that I was lying in a hospital bed and that there was no way that that was actually possible – I couldn't believe that I had just lied to Seth … what was he going to think? I didn't realise that of course I couldn't have spoken at all because I still had the trachy in. So I was telling fibs and apologising without actually saying a word. It took a few weeks before I could finally come clean on my 'lie' and it got a laugh out of everybody. The relief of waking up and no longer rolling through endless hallucinations felt amazing. The realisation of my new reality on the other hand was no less horrifying.

* * *

Lying in the hospital bed completely unable to move or do anything for myself, in enormous amounts of pain and uncomfortable throughout, was the worst period of my life. How had I gone from being a fit, able-bodied soldier to being in a bed unable to move? I was too weak to get up and too ashamed to ask a nurse for a bedpan. I could not sleep or eat properly and my bed was permanently soaked with sweat, even though I had regular bed changes. The overwhelming pain would have me lying awake in the dark listening to the beeping machines and cries of pain from other patients and wondering why I had survived. Was this as good as my life was going to get? If so, I didn't want it. Even though I had so much incredible support, I had never felt so alone.

14. R & R

Bronwyn

My 'nest' was filled at the end of June when Cayle's close friend Roos returned from Afghanistan on two weeks' Rest & Recuperation. He had become like a son to me. We were all anxious about the reunion, but none of us was as anxious as Roos. Although Cayle was aware that the lads were heading back on R & R imminently, we took the decision not to tell him that Roos would be arriving that day because we hadn't wanted him to get stressed about it.

Roos had landed at RAF Brize Norton in Oxfordshire, where Seth picked him up and drove him up to QEHB, which gave Seth time to calm Roos down and prepare him for seeing Cayle.

Once they were inside the building, Seth texted me and I left 412 to meet them in the corridor. Roos was still in uniform and he was wide-eyed, sweating and pale.

'Hello, Tannie,' he said as I walked towards him. Roos had always called me Tannie, an Afrikaans word used as a respectful or affectionate title when addressing a woman older than the speaker.

I went to hug him and I could feel his whole body shaking.

'Calm down, Roosie,' I said, 'it will be fine. Cayle will be so happy to see you.'

'Tannie, I feel ill ... I'm shaking like a shitting dog. I stood outside with Sethy and smoked half a pack of cigarettes before I could even come inside.' He continued, 'I'm more nervous now than I was any time on tour. I'd rather run out of the back of a Chinook under fire than walk through the doors and see Cayle.'

'But why?' I asked.

'I just hope he won't resent me for not being injured. I was out there doing the same stuff but I don't even have a scratch on me.'

<u>Cayle</u>

I see Roos come in, my best mate for years, and I just knew immediately that it would never be the same. We would never serve together, train together, fight together ever again. After having done so much together, that was absolutely devastating. I knew that it was never going to get back to how it was before. I was uncomfortable and hurt and I knew that I couldn't go back to Afghan, that I couldn't be there to help. I felt that I had let the side down completely. It was very tough seeing Roos so far away from where I was supposed to be.

The following day, Shorty arrived at the hospital with Roos. Sergeant James Short was the section commander on 2 May. As with most of the soldiers in their squadron, Shorty had been wearing his helmet camera on that day and it was recording at the time of the explosion. He had been the first to get over to Cayle and started treating him before Jacko the medic took over.

Sitting in the hospital, Shorty seemed a little anxious and I assumed it was from seeing Cayle, but during the conversation, he blurted out, 'Look mate, I've got the incident on my helmet cam footage – I can scrub it now if you like or do you want it? Nobody has watched it but it might give you a bit of closure.'

I was alarmed but not surprised to hear Cayle say, 'I'll have it.'

On the other side of the room, a laptop was set up and he wheeled over and watched it for the first time, insisting that none of us except Roos view the footage with him. The volume on the computer was very low, which made it hard for us to know what he was seeing, but I could feel my throat tighten and tears pricked my eyes. Looking at him over the top of the screen, I tried to read what might be going through his mind. His expression never changed once; he didn't even flinch when the IED exploded.

Cayle

The majority of what happened is what I thought had happened. The way we moved, the way we got out of the ditch, the field, the treatment, the being semi-conscious; all of that I remember. I remember the bang, I remember the dust and mud and shit all over the place. I don't remember lying on my face, but then maybe that's because I was so dazed that I only really came-to when I had been rolled over by Shorty, at which point I was trying to then scramble over into cover. Apart from that point, that's pretty much how I remember it. I don't remember exactly what I said to Harry and the rest of the guys but apparently I was talking to them. Again, I was so dazed and confused that I was just talking to them, trying to make light of it, I believe. Apart from that it's all pretty accurate, which is quite good actually because it seems that a lot of the guys who have incidents where they don't remember anything, struggle more to come to terms with it because they have no recollection of what was going on – it's just a complete blank in their minds. So I'm quite grateful that I do remember it. Although it was horrific, I do feel like I'm quite lucky to remember what happened.

I would sit there in hospital and think, all those steps that I have taken to get to this point in my life and I stepped in that window, in that fucking bracket. All of those miles run, all of those courses done. If I had stumbled 50 yards back, would that have made a difference? There I had covered thousands of miles and I step on that narrow thing. I wished I could have an action replay and see exactly what position I was in when it happened. Rifle over here and crawling out … I mean, how is it that I have like a picatinny rail, which is on the front of the rifle, smashed into my face? And what was it that broke my neck – was it the yank of the helmet as it ripped off, or was it the rifle that hit me in the chin, or was it

the landing on the ground on my head …. where did it all come
from – what bit of it caused what? What piece of shrapnel did
that … super slow-mo it down so I could see.

That afternoon we met up in the corridor with one of the military
consultants. Cayle was recovering so fast that it seemed the date for him
to be transferred to Defence Medical Rehabilitation Centre (DMRC)
at Headley Court might be brought forward.

Headley Court, in Leatherhead, Surrey, was built in 1899 and used
as headquarters for the Royal Air Force during the Second World War.
Between 1985 and 2018 it became the Defence Medical Rehabilitation
Centre, which aimed to return all service personnel who had been
injured or seriously ill to full fitness. Its services have since been
transferred to new facilities at Stanford Hall in Nottinghamshire.

* * *

We were now into July and Cayle was still in Ward 412. He'd been
visited by a few consultants and when asked what was medically most
important to him to be addressed, his response was always, 'My left
hand.'

At 3 pm on 2 July, Cayle was wheeled away from us and down the
corridor to theatre for yet another hand operation. When we got to
see him that evening, his hand was heavily bandaged, but he said his
whole left arm was still numb. The operation needed to be done under
local anaesthetic to enable Cayle to move his hand when requested.
The anaesthetic was injected into Cayle's left armpit with the aid of
guidance from an ultrasound nerve detector, which helped ensure that
all the correct nerves were anaesthetised. Cayle had chosen to watch
the procedure, so he had been propped up enough to see what was
happening. When he told us that he had wanted to watch, I concluded
that he may not be my son after all – I do not have the stomach to even
watch a needle going into my arm, let alone a whole operation!

Cayle told us that during the procedure, the surgeon had asked him if he had any brain damage. I couldn't help letting out a giggle, imagining the look of indignation on Cayle's face, but apparently bones heal much quicker in someone with brain trauma. After having a good laugh, the surgeon explained that the bones in his hand had healed right over the wires that had been inserted during one of the first hand operations, and that he was having to make incisions on the back of Cayle's hand so that he could 'crack' the bones to pull the wires out. Cayle told us, 'It sounded like crunching on chicken bones!'

The following day Cayle was approached about starting to exercise his left hand and I was very relieved when he asked to delay it for a couple of days because he said it was too painful to move. Knowing the person he is, I had been concerned that he may try to push through the pain, which could have done more harm than good.

***

Many of Cayle's guys were still out on R & R and among the visitors was Corporal Joe Cooke. We were in the common room and I was sitting to one side while the lads were chatting when once again Cayle's incident was discussed at length. 'Cookie' told us that when the guys heard the explosion, their immediate thought was that no one could have survived it. A normal anti-personnel IED is in the region of 5 kg – the IED that Cayle had stepped on was 17–20 kg and was big enough to flip over and seriously damage a vehicle. Cookie reiterated what Roos had told us – the Taliban were heard chattering over the radio immediately after the explosion and even they were unsure of what the explosion was because the IED must have been buried for a very long time. I think it was a huge reassurance for Cayle to hear, because he had always told us that there were no ground signs of an IED having been freshly planted. This was the confirmation he'd been waiting for.

Then came the day when Bryan was transferred to Headley Court. I was unsure of what Cayle's mood would be like because I knew he would miss him. I was very pleasantly surprised to walk into the ward to find him sitting on his bed looking as pleased as Punch. Parked next to the bed was a manual wheelchair. 'I decided to ditch the electric chair for a manual one to help with my upper body exercise,' Cayle explained.

This new wheelchair was much smaller and lighter, designed for someone with the use of only one hand.

'It's not as fast as the electric one, but I'm getting used to it and I've been downstairs to physio in it,' he said.

He mentioned that the smaller wheelchair meant he had been able to access the bathroom to use the toilet for the first time since being injured. It had taken him quite a few minutes but he had managed to manoeuvre himself across from the chair to the loo seat without too much difficulty. He was so relieved to finally be able to do such a simple yet private thing on his own. He was beaming.

Soon the visitors started arriving, this being the biggest group to visit all at once. One of them was Jacko, the medic who had treated Cayle on the ground. Jacko had undoubtedly saved Cayle's life and we were heavily indebted to him.

'I wasn't sure if Cayle had lost his left eye or not,' Jacko said. 'There was so much blood pouring from his face and I couldn't see where it was coming from.'

It was a combination of the wound above his left eye and the massive injury to his mouth. The heat from the explosion had cauterised Cayle's legs, ironically saving his life at the same time because it prevented him from bleeding out.

I knew that Cayle was apprehensive about seeing his guys, but he seemed particularly quiet during this visit.

Cayle

I felt guilty. I felt like I had failed them badly. In my mind it was completely my fault that I didn't see it and I had let the guys down. It was horrible. I wasn't sure if I would get to see them again. I didn't know how they would feel about me now that I was disabled. I was just angry that it had all come to such an abrupt and painful end. The Brigade Reconnaissance Force is a very small team and with the amount of training that we had been through over such a long period of time you get to know everybody so well and I had made some amazing friends. I was hugely grateful that they all came to see me when they had the chance. They're soldiers, so they want to take the piss and they want to seem positive to make the best of a shit situation. They were just trying to be supportive and even through all of the discomfort, I really enjoyed having a laugh with them in the hospital. I know they don't feel like I've let them down. Well, I wouldn't imagine that anyway, but it's different when you're lying in a bed, thousands of miles away from where you are meant to be. It's not them who made me feel like I had let them down; it's me who made me feel like I'd let them down. They've not guilted me or told me that I was shit or 'You should have seen it', or ... they've never said anything. I suppose it's a pride thing: if I had been better and seen what was invisible, then none of this would've happened. It's ridiculous really. But it took me years to let it go.

The visits from the guys had been instrumental in Cayle's speedy recovery over those weeks. So many pieces of the puzzle of the incident had been slotted together and that, combined with what we had been able to tell him of what he had been through since arriving at QEHB and particularly the days he was in a coma, was helping him get a fuller picture of just how far he had come.

During a quiet time between visitors, Cayle attempted another solo trip to the bathroom. He was gone for a very long time and I was beginning to wonder if he was okay. I didn't want to disturb him by tapping on the door, but when he eventually unlocked and opened it, he was completely ashen, drenched in sweat, and the look on his face was one of utter defeat. Shaking, utterly exhausted and demoralised, he said, 'I've just had a bit of a breakdown, my hands were so sweaty and I'm so weak that I slipped and nearly fell off the toilet as I was climbing on. I'm still struggling to do the most simple of tasks.'

Cayle's left hand was still swollen and very tender. He was trying to keep it raised so as to lessen the blood flow to it and therefore reduce the throbbing, but it was clearly causing him unbearable discomfort. He had had a busy day and put on a brave face despite the pain, but by that evening the strain was showing. I stood by his bed desperately trying not to cry. Being a parent is one of the hardest things at the best of times, but when you look into your child's eyes and reflecting back is a combination of emptiness and immense suffering, agonising despair and unanswered questions, the helplessness is overwhelming. My maternal instinct had been to protect him but it was taken out of my hands. He had no life in his voice, no spark in his eyes. At that moment I knew that I was going to break down and I would be of no help to him. The longer he was out of his coma, the harder it was becoming for me. I glanced across at Richard, indicating that I needed to walk away, leaving him to cope but knowing that he would be better in this situation than me.

I walked out to the now quiet and darkened restaurant area, slumped down heavily in a chair and began to sob from the bottom of my heart. We had said goodbye to my sister Anthea earlier that day and I was already missing her – I could have done with a woman to speak to, to share with.

As the days drifted by, Cayle slowly started to realise that he could do things that he hadn't been able to do a couple of weeks or even days before. He had been practising hard to get some movement out of his left hand, and although extremely limited, he was slowly starting to move his fingers. He had also been determined to stretch his mouth and he was able to open it much wider now, enough to fit in a forkful of food. It made meals more exciting and talking far more comfortable. However, he realised that he could no longer whistle because he couldn't pucker his lips. Indignantly he muttered, 'Not only have the Taliban stolen my legs, but they've also stolen my bloody whistle!'

A few days later, Cayle had a surprise visit from some good friends from Dartmouth: Jon and Chris. Jon is the landlord of our local pub, the Dolphin Inn. The moment Jon walked into the ward and saw Cayle, his eyes filled with tears. Chris, a massive man of more than 6ft 5in, was clearly thrilled to see Cayle. They handed over a bag of random goodies, among them a metal whistle, a crowd counter and a can of gin and tonic. Cayle had mentioned to Seth that he had been craving a G&T after dreaming about it while in the coma. Jon opened the can, stuck a straw into it and handed it to Cayle. He sat sipping on it for the duration of the visit. The crowd counter was immediately renamed a 'tottie' counter and whenever a lovely nurse walked by, Cayle was to click on the counter. By the time Jon and Chris left, the counter already had two clicks on it and the visit had been the best of medicine for Cayle.

15. Preparation

Bronwyn
8 July 2012

Before Cayle could be transferred to Headley Court, he had to prove that he could get himself into and out of a vehicle. Together with the physiotherapist, Cayle, Richard, Seth and I made our way along the corridors to the rear entrance of the hospital where Seth had parked Cayle's car. The car had been brought from camp to the hospital a few weeks before and Seth had been driving it.

As we left the building, we were able to show Cayle where he had been brought in by ambulance on 3 May. Injured soldiers were admitted through a different entrance to avoid the public and the media. Physiotherapist Sarah had been on hand with a slide-board, which Cayle tried to use, but he found it easier just to lift himself into the car. After a few successful transfers it was decided that we should take Cayle for a drive.

Seth chose to give Cayle a tour and he drove around to the various places we had stayed or visited since arriving in Birmingham ten weeks earlier. Just going past the apartment was rather emotional, transporting me back to those first few weeks of the rollercoaster we were on as Cayle's condition constantly climbed and dipped. As we headed back towards the hospital, Cayle had his first view of the 'spaceship' that is the QEHB, the place where he had been cocooned while his body healed itself with the aid of so many incredibly dedicated people.

On our way up to Ward 412 we made a joint decision to stop by the ITU Critical B ward for one last visit before Cayle left for Headley Court. The reception we received was heartfelt. Cayle had kept his word and had taken himself down to ITU on numerous occasions since his move to 412. Padre had recruited Cayle to encourage other injured service personnel who were just starting their journeys and he'd regularly been called on. The staff would definitely miss him.

* * *

Cayle's last full day at QEHB was 10 July 2012. He had been very subdued for a couple of days and I wondered if it was a combination of the insecurity of having to move to an unknown place, plus knowing that a whole new life had to start outside of the confines of those hospital walls.

We were with him during the morning doctors' rounds when the offer to show him all the medical photographs taken of him since his arrival at Role 3 hospital in Camp Bastion was made. We had told Cayle on numerous occasions how phenomenally well his body had healed, but he had nothing to compare with what he now saw. He accepted the offer.

Giving us permission to remain in the room with him, a nurse returned with a computer on wheels. I'm not quite sure what any of us had expected, but obviously these were the actual photographs, exceptionally graphic and very different from the X-rays we had recently seen.

The nurse began flipping through the images, explaining as she went. I started to feel very light-headed and had to reach out to hold onto the edge of the table next to me. The enormity of what he had survived was shown in all its horror. Of course I had seen him with my own eyes when he was brought in from Afghanistan, but by then he had already had many hours of surgery. What we were viewing was the raw truth of what he looked like immediately after the blast. I swallowed hard to stop the sobs, my eyes riveted to the screen. It was shocking to be transported back to those first days, yet at the same time it was remarkable to see the progress he had made and the miracle of the human body's ability to heal itself.

Of particular interest to Cayle were the photographs of his left hand. He had complained so much about what his hand looked like, and although we had already seen the X-rays, when he saw the graphic photographs of the state it was in when he'd arrived at QEHB, he realised what an incredible job the hand surgeon had already done. It was the same for his face, which was still a work in progress.

Sobered by the experience, we decided that it must be time for coffee and we headed downstairs to Costa. Nerves jangling, I watched as Seth went outside for a cigarette, Cayle wheeling after him. Slightly rattled, Seth took a cigarette out of the pack and Cayle, despite not being a smoker, asked for one too. As Seth looked quizzically across to Cayle, I overheard, 'Just give me a fucking cigarette!'

16. Headley

Bronwyn
11 July 2012

Ten weeks to the day after Cayle's incident, he made the biggest move so far, the one to Headley Court.

I was able to be with Cayle at QEHB from early that morning and it was with great pride that I watched the various medical staff come to bid him farewell, hearing things like, 'I don't normally do this', as he was handed greeting cards with good wishes.

With an enormous bag full of medication under my left arm, an envelope of future appointment letters in my right hand, and a huge smile on my face, I walked out of the hospital beside the Military Liaison Officer (MLO) as he wheeled Cayle through the front doors to his vehicle. We drove away and I glanced back at the building that had been such a massive part of our lives for so long. Richard, Seth and a few of the boys' friends were driving down separately and would meet us at Headley Court.

Midway through the trip, the MLO stopped at a service station to buy a few refreshments, insisting that we go inside with him. Away from the hospital, this was Cayle's first interaction with the public and he was uncomfortable with the stares he got, which he undoubtedly took as pity. He reluctantly chose something to eat, keen to get out of the building as soon as possible and back into the safety of the vehicle. Just then an elderly gentleman approached us. He offered out his hand to shake Cayle's and with some reticence Cayle took hold of it. A brief conversation ensued, with the man expressing his gratitude to Cayle for the sacrifice he had made. Shaking Cayle's hand before leaving, he pressed a £20 note into his palm. Cayle glanced up at the MLO, who urged him to take it. Cayle seemed stunned and embarrassed.

We moved towards the exit and the MLO explained that people are sometimes unsure of how to respond or show their gratitude, so their instinct is to give a donation.

Back in the car we were each lost in our own thoughts. As we drew nearer to our destination, winding our way along the beautiful tree-lined roads towards Headley Court, Cayle stopped talking altogether.

When we arrived, to my relief we found that the others were waiting for us and their presence helped to lighten the mood. We entered the building and immediately met up with Bryan. Some inevitable bantering followed and Bryan told us that he was leaving to go home to Ireland for the weekend. It would be his first time home since his incident and he said that a big party had been arranged in his local pub with many people there to greet him. He mentioned that a cake had been made for him with the words: 'Welcome home our hero' on it. Laughing, he said, 'I don't understand people – surely I'd be a hero if I hadn't been blown up!!'

* * *

The charity SSAFA (Soldiers, Sailors, Airmen and Families Association) had offered us accommodation at Norton House, in nearby Ashtead. SSAFA provides lifelong support to serving men and women and veterans from the British Armed Forces, and their families or dependants. A six-bedroom fully adapted house with easy access, able to accommodate sixteen people, was operated by them a few miles from Headley Court (HC). This was to become our home-from-home for the next few months.

We headed over to Norton House for the night, leaving Cayle at Headley. Waving goodbye to him was heartbreaking, because we knew he wanted to be with us. Although still quite heavily drugged, he was really struggling with phantom pains and I wondered what sort of night he would have.

That evening when he was alone in his room, Cayle received a message. While back in the UK on R & R from Afghanistan, Captain Harry Amos had been to see Cayle in hospital. They had been on the ground together on 2 May and had a lot to discuss. They'd spent hours chatting alone in a private room at QEHB and I knew that it would have had a positive effect on Cayle.

Harry's text read:

Hey buddy, it's probably been a hard day for you. I've spent the last few hours thinking about what I wanted to say to you. I've come to the conclusion that one thing is for certain, and that's that you do not require any sympathy because sympathy is what is offered to weak, helpless people! So instead I want to tell you where you stand in my eyes. You are the most talented soldier and all rounded bloke that I've ever had the privilege to work with! The relationship that an officer has with his soldiers is always a funny one; some, regardless of rank, are soldiers and one's subordinates and always will be; you weren't and never could be! Firstly, because I have no doubt that you could do my job in a blink, but mainly because of your slightly crazy stare and outlook on life, your self-drive and all round skill and thoughtfulness which put you well above any of your muckers (except maybe Roos); and that's before some c*** blew your legs off! Things are different now, but those traits of yours aren't; let them take you where you need to be. In a different world, I would have sought to be your friend; having said that, we're in a different world now, and I'd like to be. You have now gone and smashed any expectations that I ever had of you and you have dealt with a fucking shit hand outstandingly; just keeping fucking going!! Anyway, that's a hell of a text ramble. I will finish by saying that I have no intention of getting out of your hair any time soon. Much love. H x

While Harry was writing his text, Seth was writing a letter of his own. Before Cayle had deployed to Afghanistan he'd treated himself to a new watch – a Suunto Core to be precise. When we saw Cayle in hospital, he was without his watch, which was not exactly surprising considering the state of his left arm and hand. Seth knew how much Cayle had loved his watch, so he wrote to Suunto on his behalf:

To whom it may concern

My name is Cayle Royce and I am a serving soldier in the UK's prestigious Brigade Reconnaissance Force (BRF). I have used Suunto products since I first began doing things stupid enough to potentially get me lost in the wilderness.

Recently on tour in Afghanistan, I was unfortunate enough to find your watch strap's Achilles heel. It would appear that when I stepped on a rather large barrel of homemade explosive, I was thrown many feet into the air. Not only did my legs decide not to land with me, but my brand new Suunto Core also decided it had had enough of this war thing and we parted ways.

Forty-eight days later when I woke up from my coma in a hospital bed in Birmingham, my brother not only had to break the news that I had spent the past few weeks on death's door, had lost both of my legs, a couple of fingers, and a large bit of my face, but also that my shiny new watch was lost to the poppy fields of Southern Afghanistan. As much as I am keen to go and look for it (and my legs), the powers that be believe this to be a bad idea.

Now that I am awake and quite keen to return to my old ways of finding myself doing stupid things in stupid places (once I've learnt to walk again!), I was wondering if Suunto would be interested in joining me on my journey (after a sturdier watch strap has been designed of course).

Just a thought.
Yours sincerely
Cayle Royce

Much to his astonishment and delight, within a few weeks Cayle had received a hamper of goods from Suunto, including a new Core watch.

17. Shame

Bronwyn
14 July 2012

Cayle's first big public outing was to the Farnborough Air Show in July and he was understandably very nervous. A total of fourteen of us from Headley Court were invited. We were driven by coach to the Aviator Hotel in Farnborough, where we met up with a handful of other wounded soldiers. Although it was an overcast day, Cayle was really struggling with the glare because his eyes were still so light-sensitive and they constantly watered.

Parked on the lawn in front of the hotel were some very flashy cars and we made our way alongside them while Richard took a few photographs of us. Despite the weather, there was a crowd of thousands and thousands of people. Moving among the throng to view the various aircraft, Richard was pushing Cayle in the wheelchair. As we inched our way along, I became more and more infuriated and saddened at the insensitivity of some people. A fraction of his former self, my son seemed no more than a shell of a human being, white as a sheet and so gaunt, with an enormous brace firmly strapped around his neck. I could understand the reactions of children, but not that of adults. Instead of stepping aside when they saw the wheelchair approaching, they would get as close as they could and blatantly stare and comment, and on more than one occasion the wheelchair had to be forcefully pushed into the ogling crowd. He had been through so much and now this added humiliation on top. I found it very hard not to stare back with disgust in my eyes and I had to control my urge to lash out. I kept my hands firmly in my pockets to prevent me from doing something silly.

Everything in me wanted to protect my son from this onslaught. I could not even possibly begin to imagine what he was going through, although much was articulated in his empty, lifeless eyes. He tried to keep his left hand tucked inside his jacket most of the time, and I couldn't help but notice how often he let his gaze drop to the ground, away from the relentless staring.

He had, however, conquered his first enormous challenge and he hadn't done it in a small way – he went out among a crowd of thousands. Back on the coach heading to the safety of Headley Court, I watched him out of the corner of my eye as the motion of the vehicle gently rocked him. He nodded off next to me, pale, emotionally drained and mentally exhausted. I remembered something I had recently read: 'the wounded are the footnotes of war'.

In the lounge at Norton House that evening, Cayle became quieter and quieter as he pondered the events of the day. All of us could feel our own stresses, but none of us had any idea of just what he was experiencing. He saw some photographs of himself that Richard had taken during the day and he quietly said, 'It was easier to look at the raw, clinical photographs in the hospital than it is to see these. I don't know how I am going to be able to accept that this is what I will look like for the rest of my life.'

18. Rehab

Bronwyn
16 July 2012

There was no real time to get acquainted with his surroundings as three prosthetic sessions, an occupational therapy assessment and a physiotherapy session were now part of Cayle's day at Headley Court. Headley was soon due to close for a week for a complete upgrade and refurbishment, so he needed to be assessed by the various departments and measured up for prosthetics for them to be ready by the time Headley reopened.

When we arrived back at Headley in the afternoon to collect him, he had not yet had his doctor's assessment. Moments later the consultant walked in and invited me to attend. Thinking that by now I was seasoned enough to cope, I accepted.

Cayle lay face-down on the bed and the consultant peeled the dressing away from the pressure sore on his sacrum. It exposed a deep hole with a diameter of about 80 mm; the bone was clearly visible. The gasps uttered when the dressings were removed did not fill me with a sense of reassurance. Shocked at what they saw, the nurse queried how, in a hospital such as QEHB, it was possible that the pressure sores could have been allowed to get so bad. Cayle described the state he had been in for so many weeks, his lungs and broken neck being the main issues.

The combination of the sight and the smell meant I couldn't help but gag. I tried desperately to control the urge to run out of the room, but as the consultant started to prod at the open sore, I had to excuse myself. I headed for the nearest bathroom where I sat down heavily on the toilet seat and began to weep. Anger arose in me; anger at the apparent unfairness of the whole incident, and now the added pain and discomfort that Cayle had to endure. I cried for a few moments before standing up and giving myself a good pep talk – what use was I to him by reacting like this? The damage had already been done. I wiped my eyes and, with a false smile on my face, I re-entered the room and watched as the pressure sore was packed out and a new dressing covered the hole. I was now aware of what was essentially being hidden beneath it. Whenever I thought about it, bile would rise in my throat.

* * *

Cayle had been seeking permission to come back to Norton House with us for the week while Headley Court would be closed. There was an arm-length list of issues needing to be addressed by the various medical staff before Cayle could be granted permission, one of them being that he would need to sleep on a pressure mattress. He phoned to tell me that he would not be able to stay at Norton House with us after all as one could not be acquired and the dejection in his voice made something in me jump up and refuse to accept this. I understood their concerns but I was incensed – was he expected to stay at Headley Court with just a skeleton staff and no other company? After all the excitement at the prospect of having him with us, I couldn't believe what I was hearing.

Upset, I went to tell Mike, the manager of Norton House, that Cayle would not be able to stay with us there after all. Mike's face lit up: 'Norton House recently purchased a pressure mattress at a cost of £5,500 for just this!' I jumped for joy and phoned Cayle back to give him the good news and his mood lifted instantly.

That evening, after Cayle's dressings had been changed and we were talked through his drug administration, it was time to take him back to Norton House with us. Relaxing in the lounge after dinner, it was lovely to see Cayle lying on the sofa, quite chilled and chatting away to us. He referred to his injuries and how his life had been impacted and I thought it was good that he openly spoke about it. He became pensive for a few minutes before he commented, 'It seems really strange but it feels like my legs are hanging over the arm of the sofa.'

In one of our many chats, Mike had told us that it was not uncommon for the soldiers to lose weight when they started at Headley Court due to the exercise regime. And so began our feeding frenzy. For a week we tried to feed Cayle whatever he desired in our mission to put as much weight on him as we could before his rehabilitation began in earnest.

One particular day Cayle said, 'I feel like a turkey being fattened up for Christmas!'

The problem was, he wasn't putting on any weight while the rest of us were getting chubbier by the day. Of course it wasn't the house rules that we had to eat everything that he did, but we thought it would have been rude if we hadn't. Full fat yoghurt, custard, fresh fruit juices, pork pies, cold meats, and even lovely nutty muesli became our staple diet, with the odd South African braai (barbecue) thrown in for good measure.

In an attempt to walk off the enormous amount of calories we were consuming, we took to strolling around the very affluent neighbourhood surrounding Norton House. We would take turns pushing Cayle's wheelchair and would chatter away about what the various people in the different houses might do for a living, or comment on expensive cars parked in driveways, or just on a beautiful home. We tried to mix up the routes we took so as not to get bored and one day, on our way back to Norton House, with Richard pushing Cayle, we began descending a fairly steep hill. The little front wheels of Cayle's chair began to wobble uncontrollably, which was very entertaining. That poor unsuspecting wheelchair was not meant for downhill racing and we watched it hit record speed, hurtling towards the crossroads at the bottom of the hill, completely out of control, Cayle clinging onto the armrests and roaring with laughter while Richard tried to keep tight hold of the handles. Hearing Cayle belly-laugh again after all that time was music to my ears – it reminded me of when he was a few months old and he had laughed at the cabbage rolling across the floor.

During that week, a schoolfriend of Cayle's, who was now a teacher and living in the UK, came up from London to see him. They spent hours chatting and catching up and Cayle showed him some of the footage and photographs from Afghanistan. Watching them from the other side of the room, I was struck by the polar opposite paths these two young men's lives had taken.

Listening to Cayle sharing stories over the next few days, I was reminded of how we take so much for granted. The previous night he had climbed into bed to listen to music on his iPad, only to realise that he had left his earphones on the adjacent bed. He stretched over for them but could not reach them. He had to climb back into his wheelchair, which was between the two beds, so that he could reach across to pick up the earphones, and then get back into bed. About an hour later, he needed to go to the loo, so it was back into the wheelchair and off down the passage. He got back into bed and realised that he had left the main bedroom light on, so it was back into the wheelchair again to get to the light switch and then back into bed. Finally he could settle down for the night, only to be disturbed by the pressure mattress because the motor hummed and the mattress moved constantly throughout the night.

* * *

We tried to keep our week together as stress-free and relaxed as possible, but there were bound to be moments of frustration, anger and even depression for Cayle. Part of his daily routine was having to put silicone liners onto his legs and as the silicone is almost sticky, he found it rather difficult to do with limited use of his left hand. The combination of that, the ointment he had on his hands from massaging his scars, and the cumbersome neck brace that was cutting into his shoulders and collarbones, meant that it was quite an effort for him and he would invariably be soaked in sweat afterwards. In total frustration, unable to look down at what he was doing, one night he ripped the neck brace off, revealing the cuts and scars that he still has from the brace today. We all gasped because we knew that he needed to wear the brace, but none of us dared say anything. He had always been so fiercely independent and now he had to learn how to do even the most menial tasks again: eat, drink, go to the toilet, wash dishes – they were big hurdles he needed to overcome.

The night before Cayle was due back at Headley Court, I went to sit on the floor next to his bed and he said he was having bad phantom pains. Even though it was no longer there, he said the big toe on his left foot kept getting cramp and that the arch of his right foot felt as though someone was sticking a knife into it. He spoke about how much he missed his feet – being able to feel the grass under them, the tar of the street, and just the thought of not ever being able to feel the sand between his toes on a beach again. Referring to the fact that he had been medically discharged from the Parachute Regiment because of severe stress fractures and now this, he said to me, 'My legs were always doomed, Ma.'

He had never wanted to be pitied, but he said, 'I constantly expect to wake up from this horrible nightmare.'

He apologised regularly for what he was putting us all through and I had to remind him that he had been doing what he had always wanted to do, that he was the best he could possibly be at his job, but that he had trained for three years to fight an enemy who had had at least thirty years' experience of warfare.

There was much to mourn, but he was about to embark on a new journey of exploration and opportunities.

It was our last night together in the house. After a week of feeding, it was time to get Cayle back to Headley Court. He hadn't put on any weight. The rest of us, however, would have to resort to elasticated jeans and gym memberships.

19. Seth

Cayle was always the person I blamed for everything. I was a little shit growing up; I'd always blame 'big brother' because I knew he'd take it. He wouldn't rat me out and I got used to that. I also got used to him being the big brother I needed – he was always there. At the same time, I would try to be my own person and that sometimes went quite badly, but he was always there to support me. My first real memory is of me cutting my foot open on a port bottle in the pine forest outside the house and Cayle carrying me back home.

I joined the Royal Marines because I felt like I was wasting time – I was at university and working two jobs trying to put myself through, pay for accommodation, food and everything else. Working in a bar till 2 am followed by cleaning the same bar till 5 am was always a treat. Then heading back home and getting a few hours of sleep before going into Uni was tough. I didn't enjoy my course; my course mates were often in my bar drinking and having a good time while I worked. One particular evening I was serving the guys on my course till the early hours. We had an assignment due the next day, so I thought they must have finished up early and been out celebrating the win. The following day in a lecture, those same guys all asked for an extension on the work due as they 'didn't have time to complete it'. They got their extension, and I was one of the only people who handed in that day.

University was a waste of time and a waste of money in my mind, and hearing what Cayle and Roos were getting up to made me quite jealous. I wanted to be part of something that was going somewhere. Initially I'd wanted to join the Parachute Regiment, but then meeting a few Royal Marines down in Poole changed my mind. The way that they spoke about it pushed me to make my decision because I wanted to do something high-paced. I wanted to do something I couldn't 'cheat' at because going through school, or anything I had done before, was always too easy for me. In my last year of school I didn't have to do anything. Cayle worked his arse off the whole way through his final year and he got mediocre grades; I did hardly any work and I got pretty much straight As.

I knew that if I joined the Royal Marines I wasn't going to be able to wing my way through it. I was actually going to have to work and do it properly. The Royal Marines are the UK's Commando Force and the Royal Navy's own amphibious troops. They are an elite fighting force, optimised for worldwide rapid response, and are able to deal with a wide spectrum of threats and security challenges.

When I finished my thirty-two-week Royal Marines basic training course I had fractures in my left foot, left tibia and fibula, hip and knee, and right tibia. The troop had started out with sixty recruits and ended with seventeen of us. I was one of four recruits to be awarded the diamond, given to the section commanders of the four sections in the troop. Diamonds are recruits who hold command responsibilities within the troop and will hold leadership roles when on exercise.

I went from basic training to 40 Commando, where I was given the option of becoming a driver or doing an MLAT (Modern Language Aptitude Test). I chose the latter and went up to Beaconsfield to do a Pashto Language Course: fourteen months of intensive language training, getting ready for the next deployment to Afghanistan. I was there when I got the call from Mom letting me know that Cayle had been injured.

Cayle always wanted me to deploy, but the decision had already been made for me by the time he came out of his coma. After I was told I couldn't deploy, I offered to become Cayle's full-time carer if he needed me. It didn't take long to work out that it wouldn't be necessary.

20. Richard

While the boys were growing up we kept them busy with sport and outdoor activities. We were often away camping or fishing and Cayle proved to be a proficient outdoorsman from an early age. I would regularly tell stories of my experiences in the South African Defence Force and, on most occasions, ended up in fits of laughter trying to instruct the boys in how to march in step. Cayle never tired of those stories.

In late April 2012 Cayle phoned me from Camp Bastion to let me know that he was expecting to go out on the ground for the first patrol of his deployment. I could hear that he was concerned about it and reminded him that he had trained extensively for this very purpose and to keep his head down and tough it out.

The next call I got from him was to let me know that although they had come under heavy enemy fire, his training had kicked in and he had not flinched. I was so relieved to hear him recount the details of the attack and the adrenalin rush that he experienced and yet had managed to carry out the task he was assigned to do. I could hear how pleased he was to have got this first patrol over with and survived it. I believe from that day on we all felt that it would be okay because that had been the test. I was very proud of him.

It was early evening on 2 May and I was in France at a friend's house getting ready to leave the next day to head back to Spain when I got the phone call from the MOD to tell me that Cayle had been seriously injured, was on a flight back to Birmingham QEHB and that he may not survive. I passed out when I heard the news and there was this massive buzzing in my head; everything went dark and I could hear myself wailing, almost like a scream. My van was packed and ready, so I left my friend's house and drove through the night, straight to the hospital in Birmingham.

I have never felt so helpless as I did during those first weeks while Cayle was in a coma. We were allocated times to sit with him at his bedside and being unable to communicate, or see him respond in any way to a touch or a prayer, was overwhelming. Not a day went by without a new threat arising that could have taken him from us. The rollercoaster ride of good reports turning to bad reports within hours destroyed me and I had many run-ins with the doctors. All I could focus on was protecting my son; Bronwyn was far more level-headed, so it was better that senior staff dealt with her.

Intensive care nurses are a special breed. I have rarely seen such dedication to a very difficult job, but they are true heroes in my eyes. The physical training instructors are also amazing. There was a lovely camaraderie and an understanding that they were on my side. I have an overwhelming respect for the support we received from everyone. I think back to how awful the time spent at QEHB was, but the lovely people around us helped us through – even the lady on the till in the restaurant asking how I was doing was a huge encouragement.

QEHB was newly built and with all the latest bells and whistles, and I am sure that Cayle's chance of survival was improved by the new technologies that were available. I was pleased to discover that the designers of the hospital had included a tiny little chapel on the second floor, which became a regular retreat for me. It was quiet and I hardly ever saw anybody use it, but I could go there and pour my heart out to Jesus and He comforted me there.

After Cayle was transferred to the rehabilitation centre at Headley Court I was able to stay nearby at Norton House. This allowed me to visit Cayle daily to watch his progress in learning how to live with his injuries. It was so special to be there with him when he took his first steps and see his confidence grow. When he was booked for more surgery in Birmingham I was permitted to drive him up in my own vehicle and be there to support him. It also allowed me to be able to update Bronwyn on his progress fairly regularly.

In all, I took nine months out to spend time in the UK before I felt comfortable enough to go back to Spain, knowing that Cayle was well on the road to recovery. I knew he'd be okay.

21. Reality

Bronwyn
23 July 2012

Monday, 23 July was Cayle's first full working day at Headley Court. It was also a huge day for me – it was time for me to say farewell to him.

I had been with him for almost twelve weeks, and in a way I felt as though I had run a very hard race and I was leaving just before crossing the finishing line. I needed to get back to work and try to get some normality into my life, and Cayle needed to concentrate on his rehabilitation. A friend very kindly drove up from Dartmouth to fetch me, to save me having to catch the train home. We stood in the driveway at Headley chatting to Cayle for some time; I was loath to leave him. When it was time to go, I leaned forward and gave him the biggest hug I could. I didn't want to embarrass him in front of all those moving past us on their way to various activities, but I was so proud of him.

It felt really strange arriving at home, having to face reality again.

It would also mark the last of the regular email updates I had been sending and I knew that I would miss writing them. Since the day after Cayle had been injured, every second night I had written an email update on Cayle's current condition, sometimes only getting them out after midnight. These updates were sent to a list of 100+ people worldwide, some of whom were forwarding them on to others I have never met. People would anxiously wait for them to come through so that they could keep abreast of the situation or, in many cases, so that they would know what to pray for. The responses were such a blessing and they kept me going when I needed the encouragement. I was going to miss that.

My life had to revert to being as normal as possible and on 24 July I went back to work for the first time since 2 May.

Tea in the office of the main shop was the first order of the day, and I was able to give my colleagues an update on how far Cayle had come. When it was time to head down the street to the shop I managed, I really, really struggled. And not just that day. For several days, actually weeks, I cried constantly, couldn't concentrate on anything and was probably more of a hindrance than a help. Everyone was so patient with me and I was grateful to them for their support and understanding.

Ten days back at work and I was feeling particularly emotional but knew I needed to pull myself together to do my job properly. It was the summer holidays and Dartmouth was absolutely heaving with holidaymakers clad in summer clothes and flip-flops who were mostly just window-shopping. My Saturday assistant, Danni, was with me for moral support as much as to aid me in the running of the shop. The shop was only momentarily empty of customers when a lone woman walked in leaving her husband guzzling ice-cream outside in the street.

'Good morning,' I said as she entered, but I got no response.

She proceeded to walk around the shop, making enquiries about a few items as she went. I politely answered her every question but apparently not with the enthusiasm she expected. As she went to exit the shop her husband asked, 'Did you find anything?'

Half turning back so that she knew we would hear, her response was, 'No, but they are so bloody miserable in there that you wouldn't want to buy anything anyway!'

I looked across to Danni, who seemed shocked at the woman's comment. I stood for a few moments in utter disbelief and replayed the past couple of minutes in my head. I have never been a confrontational person and would normally much prefer to let things slide. However, this time I was completely enraged.

The next moment I found myself running out of the shop and into the street to look for her. I spotted her in the crowd further down the lane and ran up behind her, tapping her on the shoulder. As she turned around, I blurted out, 'How dare you! How dare you jump to the conclusion that someone is "bloody miserable" when you have no idea

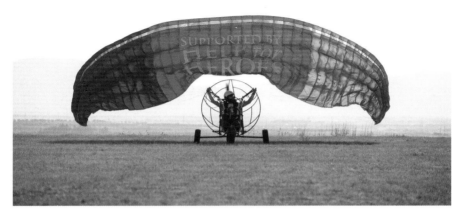

Emblem of resilience, supported by Help for Heroes throughout recovery and beyond. Photo credit Sophie Bolesworth.

Launch pad ready: Positioning the paratrike for lift-off. Photo credit Sophie Bolesworth.

Soaring high: The moment of lift-off.

Recognition: The day Cayle was awarded an MBE.

A surprise in the skies: An epic Spitfire airplane ride, courtesy of ITV and the television show 'Surprise Surprise', November 2015.

Skipper Royce: Training with his crew in La Gomera, Canary Islands, ahead of the 2015 Talisker Whisky Atlantic Challenge.

Christmas 2015: A festive celebration amidst the vastness of the Atlantic Ocean.

The Atlantic Adventure: Navigating through the tempestuous Hurricane Alex.

A Guinness World Record: The first physically disabled team of four celebrating their oceanic rowing triumph.

An embrace after 46 days at sea: Holding my salty son.

Exhaling relief: Cayle after successfully skippering his team across the less-than-ideal conditions of the Atlantic Ocean.

The pillars of life: Brothers providing mutual support throughout their shared journey.

2018: Standing in front of the awe-inspiring Victoria Falls in Zimbabwe after supporting Seth and a friend as ground crew when they competed in the 1000 mile Adventurists Icarus Trophy paramotor race across Southern Africa.

Preparation in progress: Training on the River Dart for the anticipated 2000 km kayaking journey from Seattle, USA, to Skagway, Alaska in May 2023.

Overcoming limitations: With little function in his damaged left hand, Cayle uses an Active Hands which enables him to grip the paddle.

I am the master of my fate, I am the captain of my soul.

what they are going through. I answered every question you asked me but you seemed to have a bad attitude when you entered the shop. Did it ever occur to you that perhaps there is more to the situation than what you incorrectly assumed in your two minutes in my company? My son was recently blown up in Afghanistan and he has lost both of his legs. Next time you think someone has an attitude, why don't you consider that perhaps there may be more to it than what you presume!'

Her mouth dropped open, but I never gave her a chance to respond. I swung around and ran back to the shop, shaking like a leaf by the time I got there. Danni stood wide-eyed behind the counter, never having seen me react like that to anything before. She tried to calm me down but the tears began to flow. This outburst was totally out of character for me and I realised that I was definitely no closer to dealing with the trauma of the previous few months.

Six weeks later I had my second incident at work. I had struck up many great conversations with some wonderfully friendly folk who visited the shop. I wore a 'Help for Heroes' wristband and on this particular day a man in his sixties had come into the shop. On approaching the counter he noticed my wristband and made a comment about it. I explained that my son had recently been very seriously injured in Afghanistan. He showed absolutely no empathy when he very bluntly said, 'Well, he knew what he was signing up for when he joined the military', and with that he turned and walked out of the shop.

I was utterly shocked and enormously saddened by his response. My eyes welled up with tears and my heart was so heavy that I had to go into the office to compose myself. I could not help but wonder how he would feel if someone responded to him in the same way if a loved one of his was paralysed or seriously injured in a car accident – 'Oh well, they knew the risk when they got into the vehicle.' I hoped that in time I would be able to handle these situations better.

22. Steps

Bronwyn
1 August 2012

Thirteen weeks after his incident, Cayle walked for the first time. I was overcome with emotion when Richard sent me photographs and video footage. I felt somewhat cheated that I hadn't been there to witness it, but so grateful that Richard had thought to record it for me. While learning to walk and get his balance, Cayle would be on very short legs called stubbies. Particular care was taken because of his broken neck, but he had walked between two parallel bars.

When I spoke to Cayle that night, he told me, 'Learning to walk is immensely difficult. I had to put on these massively uncomfortable sockets and stagger around the place. But my prosthetist is very pleased with my gait and she says I should have no problems walking on full legs.'

What a massive milestone it was for him – in fact, it was a massive milestone for all of us.

* * *

Most evenings I would get to chat to Cayle on the phone and he would share with me the different things he was having to do. I found myself trying to see how I would cope if I was in his position. When he explained to me how he had to climb stairs by swinging each leg out at an angle and putting it on the next step, I would try to climb my stairs at home without bending my knees and I found it to be nigh-on impossible, my hips aching in no time. I was also trying not to use my left hand very much and that was incredibly difficult. It brought home just how different things would be for him.

Left to my own devices, I found that I was starting to struggle with the little things. One evening I had the television on and one of the adverts showed a young girl walking down a street, having been given some good news. In her excitement, she leapt into the air and clicked her heels together – and with that I burst into tears because it is something that Cayle had done so often. He would never be able to do that again. I reprimanded myself by saying that he was still alive and I needed to focus on the positives and what Cayle could do rather than what he couldn't.

***

A few weeks had passed since we had last seen Cayle. Seth drove me up to Surrey for the weekend and we were excited about seeing him again. We walked into the canteen at Headley Court and instantly noticeable was that his neck brace was finally off and that he had put on some weight. He looked so much better for it. A weekend together at Norton House revealed Cayle to be in a much better frame of mind. Richard was still staying in the house and seeing Cayle most evenings. They'd spoken in depth about all manner of things and I could tell that Richard had been instrumental in Cayle's current positive attitude.

Over the weekend, Cayle had us in fits of laughter at his antics of how he was learning to adapt to his new life. He'd always been dextrous with his hands but now just the simple task of nail clipping had become a major effort. Without the full use of his left hand, he had had to devise a way of clipping his only remaining nails on his right hand. After much contemplation he thought he had the solution. He lined up the nail clippers on his table and carefully placed one finger nail between the clipper blades and then slammed down hard with his left palm, sending the clippers flying. It did the job, although it did take him a long time to clip his five remaining nails because he spent so much time looking for and then realigning the clippers between each bash. Fortunately, Richard's engineering background meant he soon managed to build a far more effective system.

Mid-afternoon, Seth and I went across to Headley Court with Cayle for his dressings to be changed. He surprised us by coming out of his room in his wheelchair with his sockets on his lap. Leading the way across to the gym, he showed us how the sockets were fitted and then he began walking around. He has always had incredible balance and he literally now just walked everywhere without having to hold on to anything. He was throwing a rugby ball around with Seth, climbing up and down a step, and bending over to pick things up. He looked so confident after only two weeks of this new way of walking that my heart could have burst with pride as I watched him.

A few weeks later, Cayle drove a car for the first time since his incident. A driving instructor with an adapted car met him at Headley Court to test him. I spoke to Cayle that night and I could hear the excitement in his voice: 'It was very strange, driving without using my feet, but it was so good to be behind the wheel again. The instructor signed me off as competent to drive!'

He immediately began his search for a vehicle that would ultimately give him his independence.

* * *

October proved to be quite a busy month for Cayle, with an outing to Oxford added in. The text message I received was as follows: 'I'm alive, Ma :) Amazing! 12000 ft, 130 mph, 30 – 40 secs of free fall. Epic! xx.'

Yes, Cayle had been skydiving! I was thrilled for him and he sounded so pleased that he had done it. I had a feeling that it may be one of the more 'sedate' things he would be doing in the future, but it had proved to him and to me that although there are so many things he couldn't do, there would be plenty of things he could.

By now he was becoming more confident and competent with walking on prostheses. While the solid carbon fibre sockets fitted over the silicone liners and onto his stumps remained the same, the length of his 'shin' was being extended until hopefully he would be at his pre-incident height. A lot was dependent on his core strength and being able to hold himself upright – the taller he stood on prostheses, the more chance there was of toppling over.

The middle of the month saw him back up in Birmingham at QEHB for what was to be the first of his head surgeries. A skin graft was taken from the back of his left thigh, and after removing the lid of the pressure sore from his head, the graft was stapled to his scalp.

When I spoke to Cayle later that afternoon, he groggily said, 'My leg is aching more than my head! But it feels as though someone has pulled a belt tightly around my head and that the skin graft is about to pop off.'

Richard had driven Cayle up to the hospital and I was comforted to know that Cayle had him to chat to. Thankfully the skin graft took well and Cayle was discharged from hospital a few days later.

More than anything, I wanted Cayle to be able to come home to Dartmouth to recover but, due to the inaccessibility of my flat, he could not stay with me. Other options needed to be considered. Fortunately, Emma Parry of Help for Heroes had kept in touch with me since learning of Cayle's incident and she was able to assist us.

Tedworth House in Tidworth, Wiltshire, is the Help for Heroes flagship Personnel Recovery Centre (PRC). The facilities are excellent and Cayle was transferred there for a couple of weeks and I was able to spend a weekend with him. H4H, famously associated with the Invictus Games, had been incredible in their support of wounded service personnel, and this was very apparent at Tedworth House – nothing was too much bother. Invictus means undefeated or unconquerable in Latin and is the name of the famous and inspiring poem by William Ernest Henley that opens this book. It ends with:

It matters not how strait the gate,
How charged with punishments the scroll,
I am the master of my fate,
I am the captain of my soul.

23. Home

Bronwyn
November 2012

I had been searching for months for a place to move to that would be suitable for Cayle and I was becoming desperate. Brigadier Chris Dick was on the case and, from all of his contacts, he had approached the Britannia Royal Naval College in Dartmouth about assisting us. Seth had been transferred to BRNC to be closer to home and was now working at the College, which meant that Cayle was already on their radar.

Almost eight months since he had last been in town, on 14 November 2012, Cayle came back to Dartmouth. A driver brought him down from Headley Court to approve a prospective officers' quarters belonging to the Naval College. Seth and I met him outside the house, which was at the top of town. Cayle looked ill at ease, remarking how odd it felt being back in the area after so long, with so much having happened. Together with the Compliance Manager, the local Occupational Therapist and Cayle's PRO (Personnel Recovery Officer), a good look around the property confirmed that it would indeed be suitable for him once the military had made some adaptations. This was very good news – Cayle would finally be able to come home between rehab sessions.

After the house inspection, there was still time before the driver was due to fetch Cayle. Seth suggested a trip into Dartmouth to pick up a takeaway coffee from one of Cayle's favourite places, Cafe Alf Resco. I had a fluttering in my stomach wondering what was going through Cayle's head and trying to pre-empt what the reactions might be if we happened to see anyone Cayle knew. Although he never got out of the vehicle, I was quietly relieved when the few people we did meet were surprised and delighted to see him. One of those was a local builder and pub landlord by the name of Chris. Chris had happened to be driving past my flat back in March as I was waving goodbye to Cayle in the church square; seeing my tears, he had realised that Cayle was leaving for deployment. He had nodded at me in acknowledgement as he drove by.

Now, as Seth parked up and climbed out of the vehicle to order the coffees, he noticed Chris working up on scaffolding on the building across the street. He whistled to attract Chris's attention and then pointed at the vehicle. Chris initially seemed to grumble at Seth's beckoning and he reluctantly made his way off the scaffolding, but as he got closer to the vehicle he realised who was inside. Completely overcome with emotion, Chris began to sob as he leaned through the open window to hug Cayle. He was shaking his head and, with tears streaming down his cheeks, he had to walk away. Composing himself, a couple of minutes later he came back and said, 'Right, enough of that! How the hell are you?'

We weren't in town for long before the driver phoned to arrange a collection point. It had been long enough for Cayle's first visit to town and for him to get an inkling of just how much people had missed him.

24. Medals

Bronwyn
December 2012

The beginning of December was a big week for Cayle and his Regiment. It was the Light Dragoons' welcome home march through Dereham town in Norfolk on Wednesday 5th, and their medals parade on Friday 7th. Cayle was understandably very apprehensive about being back on camp and among 'his' guys. Captain Harry Amos had driven down to Headley Court to pick him up and I was pleased that Cayle would have some time alone with Harry on the long drive over. Seth and Rich were unable to take time off work, so I went separately with Roos and met Cayle, Harry and Richard at the local hotel where we would be staying. It was great to see our VO John Jarvis there, as we had not seen him since just before Cayle was discharged from QEHB at the beginning of July.

The following morning Roos fetched Cayle from the hotel and drove him over to camp. Cayle needed to get back into his room to clear out his belongings. He was dreading it and I knew it would be a stressful time for him.

When I saw him that evening he looked drained.

'Being back on camp is one of the hardest things I've had to do, Ma,' he told me. 'Seeing all the guys and having to accept that this will no longer be my life.'

I knew that ultimately it was a positive thing that he had been back to camp as he needed some closure and I was grateful that it was with Roos's support. Over dinner I asked him if he was going to do a full clean shave before the parades as he had grown massive sideburns, to which he replied laughing, 'No! What are they going to do … make me stand guard?'

On the morning of the march, a freezing wind was blowing through Dereham, though thankfully it was dry. We were driven into town to await the arrival of the Regiment. I was overwhelmed by how many people had lined the streets to support and cheer. Many of the officers who had been to QEHB to meet us in the first dark few weeks after Cayle was injured walked over to greet us. Those who had already seen Cayle in camp the day before expressed their wonder at his progress.

It wasn't long before we could hear the military band coming down the street towards us. My whole body was instantly covered in goosebumps, my heart pounding in my chest in anticipation. Colonel Sam Plant led the way and it was immensely emotional watching the procession. Ahead of the Regiment was Cayle, being pushed in his wheelchair by Roos. It was a moment of huge pride and heartbreak all at once. I could read my child's face and I just knew that he wished he could be marching with them. Many supporters passed comments to Cayle, and I was pleased to see that he did smile a few times, although I couldn't be sure if it was through gritted teeth.

The Regiment, dressed in MTP (multi-terrain pattern, or camouflage), came to a standstill in front of where we were, next to the podium. After a speech by Major General Stewart, throughout which I barely took my eyes off Cayle, the march continued down to the local church where a service was held. It was then time to go to the town hall for drinks and a meal that had been supplied by the town. Cayle was completely mobbed most of the time, with the guys elbowing in to see him. He remarked afterwards, 'I think I must have done more handshaking than a Royal!'

I know that he was grateful to everyone who had made the effort to seek him out and greet him.

With a day's break between parades, Richard offered to drive Cayle and Roos up to Birmingham to collect Cayle's new car. He had spent a considerable amount of time researching to find a vehicle that would be able to carry all the equipment he was hoping he'd soon be able to make use of. He settled on a charcoal grey VW Passat Estate with all the bells and whistles. The car had been ordered back in October and, after all the adaptations had been done, was now finally ready for him to collect.

After a brief overview of the adaptations, Cayle drove the three-hour trip back to Norwich with Roos on board and Richard following closely behind. Cayle seemed totally different when he got back to the hotel – there was a definite sparkle in his eyes as he no doubt felt the freedom of his independence.

That bleak Friday morning brought rain and light snow, not exactly what was needed for a medals parade on an exposed parade ground. Cayle was up early to be at camp for rehearsals. It was bitterly cold and a brisk wind blew. With having to get himself around in his wheelchair, his hands were icy and the wet ground was contributing to the tough going. Yet another recent operation meant that his left hand was heavily bandaged and it constantly needed redressing. After parade rehearsals, Cayle had to change into his formal uniform for the 11 am parade. Unsure of what to do with all the extra trouser fabric, he neatly tucked it under his stumps.

For us, it was meeting-and-greeting while on the way to our seats. Among those at the ceremony was the ever-supportive Chris Dick. Undercover in tents with other families, we were placed in the front row, which gave us a full view of the proceedings. The parade began while the rain drizzled down. When I saw Roos wheeling Cayle across the parade ground, both of their heads held high, I had such mixed emotions. Immense sorrow, aching grief, but most of all overwhelming pride. Cayle had so looked forward to the day when he would stand alongside his comrades on parade to receive recognition for the vital role they had played in Afghanistan in Operation Herrick 16. It wasn't meant to be like this.

From where we were seated, we had the perfect view to be able to watch as Major General Stewart made his way along each row, stopping to have a few words with every man while presenting them with their medal. Coming to the end of a row closest to us, he stopped in front of Cayle. They spent some time chatting before Andrew shook Cayle's hand and presented him with his medal, pinning it to his chest. The look in Cayle's eyes was unforgettable.

After the closing march-past, we were guided to a heated hangar for a reception. Throughout, I glanced regularly over at Cayle. I watched in fascination his interaction with his peers. This for him was bittersweet, knowing it would be the last time he would be 'one of the guys' on camp. His bright future with the Army had been stolen from him, and the uncertainty of what his new future held lay ahead.

The day drew to a close and, with a final farewell to the guys, Cayle drove the 160-mile trip to Norton House where we spent the night. It was the first time since pre-injury that I had been driven by him. He had always been a competent and confident driver and nothing had changed.

The following morning he drove us on to Dartmouth. True to his word, Chris Dick had put feelers out and made some enquiries locally and a holiday apartment in the Dart Marina was made available for Cayle, the costs of which were covered by the Light Dragoons' Home Headquarters. Even so, Cayle wanted to go back to my Anzac Street flat first.

Seth, who was unable to be at the ceremony with us, was waiting outside when we arrived. He knew that accessing the first floor up the very steep, narrow staircase would be extremely difficult for Cayle, even more so with his tender hand. The bond between my sons had only strengthened over the past seven months. Quickly they worked out the best way, and with Seth's Royal Marines training, he had no problem piggy-backing Cayle up the stairs. I stood at the front door looking up and a memory flashed through my mind – when Seth had sliced his foot open on the discarded port bottle at the age of 4, Cayle had carried him to the farmhouse on his back. The roles had been reversed.

It was so good to see both of my boys sitting together in my home after almost nine months. Cayle had brought his new prosthetic legs with him, and told us that his prosthetist had now extended his legs so that he would be at his pre-incident height of 6 foot. We asked him to put the legs on so that we could see how he looked. In anticipation we watched as he rolled the silicone liners onto his legs and slipped on the carbon fibre sockets. When he was ready, Seth stood in front of him and took Cayle's hands, pulling him up to a standing position, at which stage we all burst out laughing. Clearly the prosthetist had miscalculated – Cayle was now taller than 6ft 3in Seth!

The ensuing banter was hilarious and the look of total indignation on Seth's face at the thought that Cayle would now be taller than him was a sight to behold. Cayle was quick to explain that it was hard enough walking on prosthetic legs (300 per cent harder than walking on natural legs) while trying to balance – he definitely didn't need the extra height.

Cayle impressed us by walking around the flat for a short while, the effort of which was visible, before removing the prosthetics. Peeling the liners off, there was blood all over his left stump. He carefully shuffled his way on his backside across the lounge floor to the bathroom where we washed the stump down. The top of his stump had split open. It wasn't the first time either – the last time it had happened, he wasn't able to walk for weeks. He was obviously gutted about it as he had been hoping to do a lot of walking over the upcoming weeks. Seth, determined to locate the source of the problem, prodded and poked until a rogue staple was found in the fold of the stump. It was expertly extricated, but after the 'procedure', Cayle said he would need to wait for a couple of days before attempting to walk again due to the high risk of infection with an open wound.

25. Dartmouth

Bronwyn

Being back in Dartmouth was the boost Cayle needed to feel part of the community again, and the support was amazing. The Dart Marina apartment was totally accessible for him, unlike my flat, so it meant that he could be completely independent. It was close enough to the centre of town for him to be able to wheel in whenever he wanted to. I knew he had been concerned about the reception he'd have but the responses were all positive and most people shook his hand or hugged him. The proximity of the apartment also enabled him to have visitors and there was a constant stream of people lining up to see him.

Despite it being mid-December, Cayle still struggled with overheating and he continued to wear shorts and t-shirt every day, much to the shock of everyone he met on his daily travels. He regularly had to explain that with less body for his blood to circulate around, plus the major role our feet play in our body's cooling-down process, his internal thermostat was broken.

Roos was on leave at the time and as Seth was now permanently based in Dartmouth, Cayle had all the support he needed. It wasn't long before he seemed a bit more relaxed about getting around town on his own. I felt certain he internalised a lot, but outwardly he appeared to be coping well.

With his first post-injury Christmas approaching, Cayle developed a bah-humbug attitude. He refused to have a tree or decorations in the apartment and no amount of persuasion was going to change his mind. He did, however, make regular visits to The Dolphin Inn to meet Rich, and landlord Jon took to secretly hanging a bauble on the back of his wheelchair every time he went in. His chair soon looked like a

Christmas tree – it even had a miniature tree hanging off the back and strings of blue flashing lights wound around the wheels. What a festive sight he was, weaving off down the embankment towards the apartment after a night out.

Added to this were the things he did on his own – he went kayaking on the River Dart with Nick Arding. Nick is an ex-Royal Marine GC who was working for the charity Battle Back. Hearing about Cayle and his adventurous nature, Nick was itching to get Cayle out onto the water again. When I saw Cayle shortly afterwards, he was beaming and talked about the experience with excitement in his voice. I later received an email from Nick headed 'Awesome bloke', and the first line read: 'Had a great paddle with Cayle this morning – he is amazing!!' The two of them have remained friends.

The week before Christmas, my sisters Janice, Michelle and Anthea flew in from South Africa. Michelle's husband, Keith, and their two teenage daughters joined them. Neither Keith nor the girls had seen Cayle and Seth since mid-2006 when they'd emigrated; they were understandably nervous about what to expect and unsure how to act as naturally as possible around Cayle. He soon put everyone at ease when they realised that although he may be missing some bits, he was still the same person. Before long he had everyone laughing. The bond between Cayle and Keith has always been a special one with them both being so adventurous, plus the added dimension of being in the military. It was great seeing them bantering within a short time, no strain at all between them. It was a happy reunion for Janice and Michelle too, because the last time they had seen Cayle we weren't sure whether he would survive.

While the family were with us, Cayle became our chauffeur and tour guide, and what a great one he was. Over the years he'd lived in Dartmouth, he had taken the time to learn some of its history and that of the surrounding area, which meant we got full commentary as he drove us around. It did bother me that once we got to most of these places he couldn't always participate with us. I remember staying in the car with him once when everyone got out to explore.

'Thank you for driving us all over the place but I'm just so sorry that you can't join us,' I said.

'Mom, just because I can't get out of the car and do what you're all doing doesn't mean that you guys can't enjoy yourselves. I'm just happy that I can be with you.'

We celebrated Christmas twice that year; the first on 24 December with Rich and his family when they came to the apartment for an evening of cocktails and festivities, and a more traditional Christmas the following day with our family.

Having spent a wonderful and healing few weeks together, the family flew back to South Africa after New Year; I felt very grateful for each and every one of them.

26. Anniversary

Bronwyn
2 May 2013

A year to the day since Cayle had been injured. I realised I had been anxious for the few days leading up to the anniversary. It's common knowledge that first anniversaries of life-changing events are the hardest. There had not been a single day in the past year that I hadn't cried, and even though Cayle was on leave from Headley Court and back in the Dart Marina apartment at the time, I knew he was not the person I needed to share my thoughts and feelings with.

I arranged an early morning phone call with Mike from Norton House. Speaking to him helped me immensely as he had so many positive things to say about soldiers who had been injured, how far they had come, and what they had done since.

'It might be hard for you to see now, but over the next few years he'll start doing some crazy stuff and the anniversaries will be less painful. Just watch, even a year from now he will have achieved so much.'

I spent much of the morning at work wondering how Cayle was coping, and when I went across to the apartment during my lunch break, I found him sitting in his wheelchair staring out at the river. During the entire forty-five minutes I was with him, other than the normal hello-how-are-you greetings, he never uttered a single word. I cast my mind back to those first few days when his body lay shattered in ITU, yet the bed he lay on literally shook with the ferocity of his beating heart.

Thankfully it was a busy afternoon for me at work, but when I returned to the apartment at the end of the day Cayle was gone. A fleeting moment of panic was eased when he messaged to let me know he was having coffee with a friend.

I climbed into bed that night and put things into perspective. Considering that Cayle was in a coma for forty-eight days, lost approximately 30 kg in weight and was as weak as a kitten for the following month, he had come a very long way. From kayaking in September, skydiving in October and driving his new car in December, I wondered what he might achieve in the next few years. He'd already done more since being injured than the average able-bodied person does in a lifetime.

This had been my perception of the first post-incident anniversary. I wondered whether perhaps I had been too sensitive to the occasion. The truth was, Cayle had been out drinking with Jon Pope and Rich Baker in the Dolphin Inn until all hours of the morning. He got home at 6 am and he was extremely hungover the following day. That made me smile.

27. Independence

Bronwyn
May 2013

The military pulled out all the stops and exactly one year and a day after injury, Cayle received the keys to the adapted military house. He would finally be able to unpack his bags and have a place to call home. I was making the move with him, although I was under no illusion that it would be for any personal caring duties – he was more than capable of taking care of himself. He was also very proficient in the kitchen and I knew his cooking skills far outweighed mine. My 'duties' would include cleaning, specifically the compulsory scrubbing and sanitising of floors (particularly the wet room), gardening, and the occasional kitchen duty should Cayle have to undergo a medical procedure and be unable to cook for himself.

Always one to try to keep things light, when Cayle and I went to do our first big grocery shop for the new house, he was in his wheelchair and I was pushing the trolley. Coming towards us down the chilled aisle was a man pushing a trolley with two young girls in it and a young boy walking alongside. The two girls saw Cayle and quietly asked their dad about the wheelchair and he gently began explaining that Cayle must have been injured in some sort of accident. The young lad interrupted his dad by blurting out loudly, 'What happened to his legs?'

Cayle, casually deciding which flavour of yoghurt to choose, responded just as loudly, 'It's because I didn't eat my vegetables.'

The shock on the boy's face was priceless, but his dad gave Cayle a thumbs-up and we chuckled as we passed each other in the aisle.

For the first few weeks after we moved into the military house, Cayle didn't have a wheelchair to use upstairs, which meant that once he was up there via the stairlift, he had to shuffle around on the floor on his bum. One evening he was sitting on his bed doing some work on his laptop when he remembered that he needed to tell Seth something, who happened to be in the adjacent room. I was in the lounge at the time, directly underneath Cayle's room, when I heard a hefty thump.

'Everything okay?' I called out.

No response came, so I went upstairs to investigate.

'I literally just stepped off the bed,' said Cayle, 'I completely forgot that I don't have legs!'

* * *

When Cayle had been flown back to the UK after the incident, his personal belongings were put onto the C-17 with him, but they mysteriously never made it to the hospital. Months of investigation and searches led nowhere and we eventually gave up hope of ever finding them. A couple of months after moving into the house, he received a call to say that his goods had been located and were on their way to him. A massive cardboard box was delivered to the house and, with Seth's help and me standing by, Cayle began unpacking it.

I could not have been more grateful that Seth was with us. Memories came flooding back for Cayle as he found things like the watch he had been wearing at the time of the incident. He thought it had been destroyed by the blast but the evidence here in front of him showed that it had been cut off his wrist. It was still covered in his blood and the mud from Afghanistan. Also in the box was his day sack, completely shredded down the left hand side, the straps broken where it had been blasted off his body. Most of the kit he had been wearing on that day was not there because it had been completely obliterated. As Cayle reached further down inside the box, I thought back to the evening he had been injured and my distress at the prospect of his boots being sent back to us. Now as he pulled boots and socks out of the box, he was making jokes with Seth: 'Well, I won't be needing these anymore – just as well you wear the same size!'

Without even realising he was doing it, he totally diffused the situation for me. I considered the fact that perhaps it had been a blessing in disguise for us all that his belongings had been lost for the past year, each of us now maybe slightly more able to cope.

* * *

Cayle had yet more hand surgery at Salisbury hospital in June 2013. He drove himself home, earlier than expected, and he seemed very agitated and rather curt. I put it down to the pain he was in but as the evening progressed and he had a few beers inside him, he started to divulge a little. He wheeled himself over to me and began to chat. In front of me on the table was a goodie box, which I had wrapped ready to send to the boys' cousin who was on deployment in Afghanistan at the time. Goodie boxes are seen as a valuable contribution in boosting morale among Armed Forces serving on overseas operations.

He stared at the parcel for a long while before finally asking, 'What's inside it?'

I reeled through the contents.

'I loved getting your parcels.' he said. 'They were something to look forward to when we got back to Bastion after an op. They were always filled with some really random things, but the best were your baked goodies … rusks, crunchies, fudge. The guys loved them too.' He smiled weakly.

A few moments of silence followed and, obviously lubricated by the beers he had been drinking, he told me, 'I just want to go back, Mom. I want nothing more than to go back to Afghan and finish the job. I loved being out there and it was cut short.'

He continued, 'I let the guys down. I put their lives in danger because I stepped on that thing. I wanted to complete the tour so that I could apply for selection and go down the Special Forces route. I chose the British Army because I always wanted to go and do the Halo jobs.'

We both cried as he poured out his regrets and extreme sadness at what he perceived to be lost opportunities.

28. Confidence

Bronwyn
August 2013

At the end of July 2013, I was surprised to receive an email asking if I would be prepared to be interviewed and photographed for *Good Housekeeping* magazine's Bumper Christmas Issue. They had learned about me through the charity SSAFA (Soldiers, Sailors, Airmen and Families Association) and were keen to get me involved. I initially politely declined because I felt I didn't have the confidence to pull it off, but a friend encouraged me to change my mind, saying that I should take my example from Cayle and think about the people I might be able to inspire through the article. I agreed to go ahead and in mid-August I found myself on an early morning train up to Paddington Station in London, where I was collected by a driver and taken to the Grosvenor Hotel. Just stepping into the beautifully plush hotel reception was amazing and I was instantly pleased I had gone. My day was packed with pampering and treats, starting from the moment I walked through the doors. Most people have had, at one point or another, frivolous daydreams about being faced with free choice of anything their heart could desire. This room, filled with literally hundreds of dresses and pairs of shoes, made this particular dream a reality. Hair and make-up done, I could hardly believe what a difference a professional makeover, a beautiful red dress, some staggeringly high heels and a good photographer could make.

The article was titled 'True Heroines' and the opening statement read:

The courageous women and men who put their lives on the line
for our country make sacrifices every day – as do their families.

At this time of year, our hearts go out to those serving far from home, the children who miss their parents, and the Forces mothers who can't sleep for worry, but still support the troops however they can. To give these families a very big thank you, *Good Housekeeping* brought five wonderful women to London for a luxury break and a makeover. They really are heroines worthy of the name, and we wish them, and all of you, a very happy Christmas.

Each one of us had a few photographs published in the magazine, together with an outline of why we were considered a heroine. The whole experience gave me a little confidence boost, a push to start believing in myself a little more, and I was astounded at the positive response to the article. Hearing the feedback from the people whose lives it had touched was confirmation for me that I had made the right decision.

29. Challenges

Bronwyn
2013

In February 2013, Cayle had gone to Bavaria on a skiing trip with a group of wounded servicemen. Not only was it his first post-incident skiing trip, but it was the first time that he had been on a plane since the flight back from Afghanistan. It hadn't even crossed my mind the issues he would encounter when flying. When it came to sitting on the plane, he realised just how small the gap is between the seats – the carbon fibre sockets are longer than the gap, which meant that he spent the duration of the flight with the ends of the sockets wedged against the seat in front, while he propped himself halfway up the back of his seat. He'd been advised not to remove his prosthetics during the flight because the change in altitude would cause his stumps to swell and he would not be able to get the sockets back on when they landed. Despite the flights, he greatly benefited from the trip and it underlined that his new life need not be so different from the old.

Five months later and barely a month after hand surgery, Cayle left for the US with a group of wounded British soldiers to participate in Soldier Ride, a four-day event where he hand-cycled with approximately fifty members of Wounded Warriors, the American version of the UK's Battle Back, starting in New York and ending in the Hamptons. Cayle said the whole ride had been an incredible experience and they had cycled approximately sixty-eight miles over three days.

He came home buzzing and totally invigorated by the trip. Little did I know what was yet to come.

30. Row

Bronwyn and Cayle
Mid–2013

When Cayle was still in QEHB in 2012, Captain James Kayll had gone to visit him and, as they had done some sailing together previously, James was keen to get Cayle out onto the water again.

Cayle had expectations of grandeur, perhaps a luxurious 100-ft yacht with bikini-clad girls serving cocktails. Being an impoverished army officer, however, James's proposal to Cayle, via telephone in April 2013, was something entirely different.

<u>Cayle</u>

I was approached by James Kayll, who said, 'Mate, do you want to go and row the Atlantic Ocean?', and I kind of went, 'What? This is ridiculous … yes, of course, absolutely!'

The Talisker Whisky Atlantic Challenge, known as the world's toughest rowing race, was to commence in the first week of December 2013 from San Sebastian Port in La Gomera in the Canary Islands and end 3,000 nautical miles across the Atlantic Ocean in English Harbour, Antigua. The race, expected to take anything from fifty to eighty days to complete, is a totally unsupported crossing. James would be the skipper of the Row2Recovery crew and the other two team members would consist of one disabled and one able-bodied soldier. Working in pairs, they would be rowing two hours on and two hours off for the duration of the crossing.

When Cayle sat me down to share the news, Seth was sitting alongside him for support (I suppose more for me than for him). I obviously had a minor panic, but I had a sense that this challenge would be instrumental in his recovery. We chatted a bit about the row but I don't think the enormity of what he was proposing had registered with me. I hugged him and reminded him of the conversation we'd had when he was not long out of his coma – he had wondered what he would be able to do, and I had told him then that doors would open and he would have the opportunity to do things that otherwise would not have been available to him. What I did know was that this would be the start of much bigger things.

Cayle

It was important for me when I first got injured to see that people in a similar position to me were still doing this kind of stuff – this is the kind of stuff that I live for. Waking up in hospital with no legs, one hand and half your face blown apart makes you question what the future might look like. It makes you wonder whether the adventure is over. Getting involved in this kind of expedition gives you something to aim for and instils confidence that you can still get stuck into seriously challenging things. I have seen first-hand the positive impact that this kind of thing has for giving hope to those who are going through their rehab. It plays a huge part in regaining your independence.

Preparations for the row were well underway as the departure date grew closer. Cayle was spending a lot of time away from home, travelling all over the country to various venues for media interviews, boat equipment training, collecting supplies and packing the boat ready for shipping. There were courses to be done, including a Yachtmasters' course that he passed with an incredible 99.9%. I watched Cayle's confidence grow as the bombardment of media coverage pushed the crew into the limelight.

In early November 2013, the pressure to have everything ready for the row was mounting. Cayle was sitting on the sofa at home with his iPad on his lap and his wheelchair alongside him. I knew he was busy sorting out stuff for the row and he looked a little frustrated about something. Without thinking, I walked over and sat in his wheelchair to chat to him and then the realisation hit me: 'This is the very first time I have ever sat in your chair!' I said, almost in a whisper. It was the strangest feeling.

He picked his head up and said, 'Please will you make me a cup of coffee, Mom.'

As I went to get out of his chair, he said, 'Try making it from sitting in the wheelchair.'

I clumsily manoeuvred the wheelchair past the sofa and through the doorway but not without first connecting with the door frame. When I finally got to the kitchen I literally saw things from a different angle. Just those few moments had given me a minute glimpse into the wheelchair life my son lives and I felt rather emotional. I made the coffee and then I had to get it to him. I attempted to put the cup of boiling hot liquid between my knees just as he did but it was scalding my legs. I wrapped the cup in a tea towel before carefully wheeling my way back to the lounge, trying my utmost not to burn myself or spill any of it on the way. This five-minute role-play gave me a massive new respect for Cayle, who copes so ably without complaining.

On Sunday, 17 November 2013, I said farewell to my courageous, determined son. The next contact I had from him was the following night when he messaged to let me know that they were all safely in La Gomera and sitting in the Blue Marlin pub, having a beer and meeting some of the other crews. He said the atmosphere was fantastic and he could feel friendships and camaraderie building, the thing he'd missed the most since leaving the military.

The following two weeks consisted of readying both their boat and themselves for the row. I was very grateful that Richard had made the decision to travel to the island and he remained in La Gomera for the duration of the crew's preparation. His marine experience and knowledge made him invaluable to the Row2Recovery crew in sorting out glitches with the boat – and there were many. Richard had an understandable interest in sorting out any issues for Cayle, including the changeover between shifts of Cayle's static seat to Scott's sliding seat. The fixtures on the seat were very fiddly and had made the changeover quite laborious and tricky, but he was able to simplify it for them. He also helped solve the problem of the lack of grip on the oar of Cayle's damaged left hand, among many other seemingly minor issues that could potentially become much larger problems out at sea where they would be more difficult to fix. The Row2Recovery boat would be far better prepared for the journey ahead because of Richard's input. Another bonus was that I knew Richard would be far less emotional when it came to the departure than I would have been, and ultimately that would be much better for Cayle.

Cayle phoned me on the morning of 4 December from the jetty, amid a flurry of microphones and TV cameras being shoved towards him, as he was about to board their boat, *Endeavour*. We said our farewells and I managed to hold myself together while we spoke. I told him how proud I was of him and of the distance he had come in such a short time. He sounded excited and apprehensive but keen to get going, and said he felt very prepared for what lay ahead. I cried as soon as the call ended, but this time more from pride than concern.

At 1 pm the horn was sounded and the Talisker Whisky Atlantic Challenge began. The tracking device on each of the sixteen starting boats immediately became active and, with the tracking app being regularly updated, I felt somewhat comforted. I became addicted to tracking the race and I found that I was waking every few hours during the night to get the latest update. It was fascinating, watching the tactics of each team as they chose their own course in their quest to reach the finish line, 3,000 nautical miles away in Antigua, in the shortest possible time.

I flew out to Cape Town to spend Christmas and New Year with my family and we spoke constantly about the fact that while we were out for a meal, or off to spend a lazy afternoon at a wine farm, or even just at home having a cup of coffee, Cayle was still rowing. It was almost impossible to comprehend the enormity of the challenge. I constantly kept my phone with me so that Cayle could reach me or in case Alex McKenzie (that year's PR for Row2Recovery and my point of contact) needed to get hold of me in the event of an emergency. During the forty-eight days at sea, Cayle managed to phone me on average once a week.

What I do recall very vividly is the anxiety I was feeling in the days leading up to Christmas. It was not unlike what I had felt before Cayle was injured, but I put it down to the fact that I would be away from both of my sons. I was in a shopping mall on the outskirts of Cape Town with my sister Michelle early on the morning of 19 December, buying some last-minute bits and pieces, when I felt my phone vibrating in my pocket. I noted that it was Alex McKenzie and my heart skipped a couple of beats as I realised that it must be important. I took a deep breath before answering the call.

'Bronwyn, *Endeavour* capsized a few hours ago in a massive storm. Cayle and James were on the oars but they're fine. They were both thrown from the boat but thankfully tethered to it. Cayle has injured his head when the oar hit him but otherwise they seem to be okay. I wanted to let you know before the media get hold of it.'

Cayle

Impact! At 00:16 we were hit from our right. And then a second wave came from the rear. The boat felt like it was pretty much vertical in the air with the stern high out of the water and I could see James way above me. It reminded me of a poster I used to have at home of a big wave surfer falling from a massive wave at Mavericks. The slogan read 'don't scream, you'll need the air'. The last thing I heard was the deafening roar of the wave and the sound of me taking in a huge breath.

As soon as we capsized, it was like being in a washing machine. I hit something with my face and I was ripped out of my seat. I swam to the surface and saw items floating in the water that had been ripped from the boat. I swam to retrieve them and then quickly realised that I should focus on 'retrieving' myself! Before I got out of the water I saw that some other kit was hanging over the side. I pushed it back in first and then got myself back in. Scott and Jenks tried to help and we told them to get back in the cabins in case we got rolled again. James was back onboard pretty quickly as we were now beam-on [side on] to the oncoming waves and he took over the hand steering to steer the boat back onto a safer course.

The capsize was far less shit than I expected. The first thought I had when I hit the water was, 'Oh good, at least it's warm.' The boat was upright before I had even got my own head above water. As soon as we were upright, James was all over it. We reported the situation immediately to the race duty officer, then we quickly checked all the kit and got rowing again straight away. It wasn't panic stations. Immediately after the incident we had a chuckle about it. The only real downer for a South African like myself is to have lost our snack packs overboard. I wouldn't have minded too much but we had fifty packets of biltong in there!

We were very fortunate that the boat hadn't been damaged, but I did discover the cause of the cut on my face – I had snapped an oar with my head. The build-up to the capsize was far worse than the actual roll. The constant thought was, 'When is it going to happen and is the boat going to right itself, am I going to get pinned underneath it due to being strapped into my seat, etc.' There was almost a sense of relief once it had happened.

Cayle had stared death in the face for the second time and survived. The media had a field day and I was thankful for Alex's phone call, which had prepped me. I also realised that, oddly enough, the capsize put me slightly more at ease because after that I felt that the rest of the crossing would hopefully go without any further catastrophes.

I was back in the UK from South Africa by mid-January and as the boat got nearer to her destination, plans were made for us to fly out to Antigua. Quite unused to being in the spotlight, I found it rather daunting to be informed on arrival at the airport that Seth and I were to be interviewed by the media before flying out. My nerves got the better of me as I stammered my way through the questions fired at us, my lack of self-confidence showing. There was just enough time for a quick coffee before we had to head to the boarding gate. Our group consisted of the family members of the R2R crew and we attracted a few stares and comments as we made our way through the terminal pushing wheelchairs laden with prosthetic legs and other paraphernalia but no occupants. Eight hours later we landed in balmy Antigua and the gush of warm air as the plane door opened was enormously welcome after the chilly English winter we had left behind.

We soon settled into a daily routine of meeting up with the organisers to hear the latest news, and the excitement was building when we knew the boat was nearing the finish line.

The sun had just set on Tuesday, 21 January as we stood on the quay, amid hundreds of other people, outside the Copper and Lumber Store Inn in Nelson's Dockyard. In the distance we saw a flare shoot up into the night sky, announcing that Row2Recovery had crossed the line in fourth place in a time of forty-eight days, nine hours and thirteen minutes, although the boat and her crew were not yet visible to us. The throng around us erupted with whooping and whistling. People had come from all over the island to witness the arrival of this incredible team. English Harbour was electric with anticipation as horns blared from boats, flares glowed in the dark and a cannon was fired. The Antiguan military lined the quay and a steel band was playing as we waved flags and scanned the dark water for that first glimpse of the boat.

And then we saw the reflection of light on the oars as they rowed in. The noise became deafening as the boat got closer to the quay and the white-toothed smiles on the guys' faces showed their appreciation and astonishment at the turnout. As *Endeavour* docked alongside us, I reached out to my precious son and held his salty, hairy face in my hands. It was so good to feel him and to know that he was safe after what had been an incredible journey by anyone's standards, let alone someone with his injuries. He gave me an enormous bear-hug and a smile that I shall remember forever.

After seven weeks at sea, we had been told to expect some staggering by the rowers when they got onto solid ground. We didn't think this would be a problem for Cayle, for obvious reasons. He hauled himself into his wheelchair, but what we didn't expect was that he would fall straight out! We all laughed, no one more than him. Many Antiguan women handed their young babies to Cayle and he looked at me, surprised, saying, 'I feel a little like the Pope giving a blessing!'

The Light Dragoons had very generously surprised Cayle by flying Shorty and one of Cayle's other friends from the regiment, David Scammell, out to Antigua to be there for his arrival. It was a wonderful treat for him and you could see how happy he was to be hanging out with his guys again.

The whole area was teeming with media and the *Endeavour* crew were ushered away within minutes for interviews and photo shoots.

It was during this time that a table was set and a meal prepared for them. Before he'd left the UK, Cayle had been given a very special bottle of champagne by Captain Harry Amos – a bottle of Pol Roger that bore the emblem of the Light Dragoons. The bottle was to be carried across the ocean with him and opened on arrival in Antigua. We had arranged for glasses to be on the table and used a prosthetic leg as the ice bucket. Hamburgers and chips were eagerly consumed by the crew, with a lot of banter thrown in for good measure. The celebrations went on long into the night, although not by the crew – they had all showered and gone for an early night, sleeping uninterrupted and in proper beds.

Ten busy days after flying into Antigua, we landed back in the icy UK. Jon and Rich had organised a welcome home party for Cayle at the Dolphin Inn. Jon had decorated the pub with various photographs of Cayle and, in appreciation of his support, Cayle donated one of the oars he had used to row across the Atlantic Ocean (not the broken one!). To this day, the oar still hangs proudly on the wall of the pub, together with the photographs.

Once home, the invitations for Cayle to do motivational talks around the country began to flood in. He had inspired so many people, disabled and able-bodied, and his life continued as a testament to what is possible even after such severe injury. The Row2Recovery team's diaries filled up and they even appeared live on television. Cayle mentioned to me that the whole trip was starting to seem totally surreal.

It was interesting to note the number of comments made about Cayle's beard though, which he'd decided not to shave off after the crossing. The difference it made to Cayle's confidence was undeniable. He was a changed man, no longer avoiding eye contact or dropping his head when in public. His scars were now hidden from view. He wouldn't have to endure the relentless stares of insensitive people or be self-conscious about being 'different'. It infuriated me that some people chose to judge him because he had a full beard, unaware that it being there might be for reasons other than fashion.

31. Paratrike

Bronwyn
May 2014

Paramotor is the generic name for the harness and propulsive portion of a powered paraglider. There are two basic types of paramotor: foot launch and wheel launch. Foot launch models consist of a frame with harness, fuel tank, engine and propeller. The unit is worn like a large backpack. A wheel launch paratrike, as the name implies, is a three-wheeled unit with a seat for one or two occupants, but the basics are largely the same.

On the second anniversary of Cayle's incident, I thought back to the same time the previous year. Cayle had been struggling so much to come to terms with how drastically his life had changed. I realised that, a year on, with so much achievement under his belt, an immense amount of emotional healing had taken place. It had been a blur of activity and adventure for him, which I couldn't see ending any time soon. Mike Turner had been right when he'd said 'Give it a year'.

In stark contrast to the previous anniversary's outing, this year Cayle was introduced to paragliding and he was instantly hooked. However, paragliding solo was not a feasible option for him, so he was introduced to paratriking. It was to become a big part of his life, making me wonder what was riskiest: rowing an ocean, or flying in a fan-propelled trike with a kite hanging above it.

Cayle, accompanied by Seth, started with a trip in August 2014 up the Rift Valley in Kenya with Flying for Heroes. In October 2015, flying solo this time, Cayle took part in The Adventurists' Icarus Trophy, the first ever long-distance paramotor race – a 2,000km route heading south from Seattle, down the west coast of the USA to Valley Springs, Sacramento. Entrants for the challenge ranged from professional paramotor pilots down to complete novices. Taking Seth along as his ground crew, Cayle was able to compete against able-bodied pilots.

After meeting Cayle during the Kenya Flying for Heroes expedition back in August 2014, Kester Heynes of Parajet purpose-built a solo trike for Cayle and trained him to fly it. The assistance of Help for Heroes, who kindly bought him his rig, had opened further doors of adventure for him. While I stayed at home wondering what I had done to create these two adventure-seeking sons, I also secretly loved the fact that they both had resolved to get as much out of life as they possibly could.

A lot of media attention surrounded this event, with Cayle being summoned for yet more interviews:

Cayle

There's a definite tremor in the heart at the moment. When I realised just how massive this place is and the kind of terrain and foliage that we've got to dodge along the way, it's going to be an incredibly emotional race. You're just on your own in this little flying machine, taking in the world. You're not moving particularly quickly – they're fairly slow-moving aircraft, so you have plenty of time to just be there, be in the moment, taking your time flying from A to B and enjoying what you're flying through. You have to have that element of danger and discomfort and concern because otherwise there's no real achievement ... if you get to the end of that and you're like, 'Yes!!! I did that ... it was as dodgy as bloody hell but I got there in the end!' and you can have that beer and say to yourself ... 'I bloody did that!!'

The first weekend of the Icarus Trophy was a qualifying event and Cayle was the first in the air for the trials. I knew he was due to be flying that day and I hoped I'd hear from at least one of the boys on how it had gone; what I didn't expect was how I would find out. Sitting at home in

Dartmouth, I opened my phone and came across this Facebook post: 'Cayle's just had a catastrophic engine failure …'.

After twenty-five minutes in the air and at an altitude of 3,200ft, his engine had seized without any warning. There were 100-ft pine trees as far as he could see, which made for a less than excellent landing option. After radioing to the race organisers that he was making a forced landing out in the trees, Cayle glided over to what looked like his only landing option for miles around. There was a barn among the trees with a small, sloping grass field to put the trike down in. The trike clipped the treetops as Cayle glided in unpowered. Fortunately, he managed to slow the trike down using the wing and brought it to a stop before it ran off into the creek at the end of the field. Seth and the ground crew, having heard the radio call and following on the tracker, were with him within fifteen minutes and recovered both Cayle and the trike.

It began to dawn on me that here was the answer to my question: perhaps this paratrike thing was in fact more dangerous than the rowing.

The incredible efforts of Kester, Seth and Cayle meant that the faulty engine was repaired and Cayle was soon back in the air. The weather throughout the race was as unforgiving as the terrain. With pine trees as far as the eye could see, enormous 10,000-ft mountains to cross, and rainy squalls and heavy winds that came up out of nowhere, covering the distance in what was essentially an oversized kite propelled by a lawnmower engine was definitely a challenge. There were three major incidents during the race, resulting in one competitor with a broken arm, one with a broken leg and unfortunately one with a broken spine and shattered pelvis. Thankfully, Cayle completed it unscathed and, overall, the race was a huge success.

Cayle has gone on to do many more of these trips. He undoubtedly does these things for the adventure, and underestimates just how much public awareness of injured, wounded and sick military personnel it creates.

32. Skipper

Bronwyn and Cayle
2015

Early in 2015, Cayle was approached by Paddy Nicoll, the chairman of Row2Recovery, about doing the Talisker Whisky Atlantic Challenge for a second time – but this time as the skipper of an all-amputee crew. Cayle was away in Spain training in his paratrike at the time and would only receive this email a month later. It would be a world-first attempt for a four-man all-amputee crew to row an ocean. So began months of selections, boat preparations and the inevitable media interviews. With the final crew of Cayle plus three single amputees selected, the slogan became '4 men, 3 legs, 1 ocean'. Their boat became affectionately known as 'Legless'.

After returning from his first row, Cayle had gone back to Headley Court for further rehab. While he was there, a chap by the name of Lee 'Frank' Spencer, of the Royal Marines had been moved into the same room as Cayle.

<u>Cayle</u>

The first time I met Frank in Headley, the poor guy was so heavily drugged due to recently losing his leg and it was actually quite hard to understand him. That did not stop him from breaking out his guitar and belting out a bunch of songs that he had created though. I had no clue what was going on but it was entertaining either way. He asked why I had a beard and a tan and I explained the endeavour I'd just completed, which he commented on as being a thoroughly shit idea.

I was very pleased some months later when we ran the selection for the all-amputee crew and Frank was the first man to walk through the door. Watching him pulling on the oars in the first training row, it became very obvious that he was going to be in the crew.

After some weather delays, the 2015 Talisker Whisky Atlantic Challenge commenced on 20 December, with twenty-six boats competing. The crossing for Row2Recovery was not without its fair share of trials along the way.

Before our departure to the Canary Islands I had advised the guys that it would be a good idea to bring iPods filled with audiobooks and music to stave off the monotony of rowing. Frank and I rowed every shift together and did not plug our headphones in once. We chatted and laughed the entire way across without a single heated word. We learned poems, sang songs, star-gazed and went through just about every little detail of our lives.

At one point, about a week out of Antigua, Frank suddenly went quiet, which is extremely unusual. He had not shut up the whole way across. I turned around and asked what was wrong.

'Cayle, I literally have nothing else to tell you; we've been through everything I've got.'

'Well, make something up!' I said to him. 'I ran out ages ago – I've been making shit up for two weeks!'

We howled with laughter and shortly afterwards Frank had remembered a whole new list of things to keep us going.

We had a few close calls on the row, including Frank's prosthetic leg snapping as he went overboard. My stomach turned at the sound of it as I wasn't sure if it was bone breaking or the prosthetic. Fortunately it was the latter and he had brought a spare.

We were also hit by Hurricane Alex midway across the Atlantic. We had to deploy the para-anchor to slow our drift backwards, which is a disheartening experience. After four days of getting violently thrown around in the storm, we were back underway and making progress towards our destination.

Seth and I had flown out to Antigua in anticipation of their arrival. The last night at sea, the night of Wednesday, 3 February 2016, Cayle phoned me. I was in my hotel room at the time, preparing to go out to meet the other families for a meal. He sounded extremely stressed and said they were in very heavy headwinds.

<u>Cayle</u>

The forecast for our final twenty-four hours at sea had been a promising one with good winds and a gentle swell all the way into Antigua. Having received this great news earlier in the day, I was surprised to begin to feel a light breeze on the back of my neck. At this point we could clearly see the lights of Antigua on the horizon, so we were rowing hard to get ourselves home. Looking over my left shoulder I could see a collection of absolutely enormous cumulonimbus thunder clouds on the horizon that were flashing intermittently.

It was not long before the light breeze became increasingly stronger and the boat was being forced further south than I would have wanted. Westerly progress towards English

Harbour became increasingly difficult. My concerns only grew as the sea started to be whipped up into a frenzy and waves began breaking over the side of the boat, often knocking us from our seats.

The rain came with a startling deluge and, with it, the wind grew so strong that the boat was being blown completely sideways and away from the island. Flashes of lightning and rumbles of thunder surrounded us. Due to the severity of the downpour, from my seat, which is only about a metre away from my cabin, I could not see the cabin or the instruments that I use to navigate.

I knew that if we could just make it into the wind-shadow of Antigua, only a few miles away, the sea would be calmer and the wind less severe. There was a very real risk of us missing the island altogether and being blown past it, which, after all this time at sea, would be devastating as there would be no way to row back and we would need to be towed into English Harbour. Hardly the way we wanted to end this amazing adventure.

Our auto helm started to fail repeatedly under the strain of the storm smashing into us. Frank and I were shouting obscenities at the elements in this moment of great injustice, where it seemed like we would fail at the final hurdle. Both of us were fully aware that it would not help a bit with the weather, but it did help us to get a rage on and pull with everything we had. While I had to keep rotating with another rower to keep the boat in one piece and on course, Frank sat and rowed constantly without a stop or a change for nearly nine hours. He had proven throughout the row to be an absolute machine on the oars and a fantastic member of the crew and was fully aware that he was the most powerful rower on the boat. Without this effort I am certain that the outcome would have been entirely different. Eventually we did break into the shadow of the island and we all breathed a definite sigh of relief.

At the end of the first row, Cayle had lost far too much weight and he was determined that it would not happen again, so this time he made sure he ate something after every shift. It paid off. 'Legless' crossed the finish line on Thursday, 4 February in eighth position out of twenty-six boats after forty-six days, six hours, nineteen minutes and forty-one seconds at sea, and a very healthy and strong-looking Cayle beamed with pride when they made their way into English Harbour as he held a flare above his head.

Cayle

It is a staggering feeling, rowing into English Harbour. The overwhelming sense of relief and the incredible amount of support that we received on arrival is humbling. I am so grateful to see how many people seem to care and actively make a point of showing it. The Antiguan Army standing beside hundreds of cheering supporters, all coming to welcome us home. Coming alongside the quay and seeing my ever-supportive, beaming-faced Mom diving in to give me a hug and to kiss my salty face, and my 'little' brother, who has sacrificed so much to be there for me over the years, is the best feeling in the world.

Paddy Nicoll, who is the only reason Row2Recovery has been so successful, and has personally given so much to make this all possible, was standing there with a massive smile on his face and bottles of champagne in hand, ready to start the celebrations and no doubt heaving a big sigh of relief that we were safely ashore. I think Paddy was more relieved than we were for us to be safely in port. The number of sleepless nights that he must have had thinking of all the tragedies that may occur while we were at sea and, worse yet, having to deal with four families on shore all wanting constant updates of how everything was progressing, must have been utterly exhausting. The sacrifices that he has made to support so many wounded servicemen and women like me is unparalleled and I am privileged to call him my friend.

It was an absolute treat to have Neil Heritage there, a fellow double-amputee and ocean rower who mentored me through my first row and helped us in La Gomera to get the boat ready for departure. Too many friendly faces to name, but I am no less grateful to those who showed up.

Antigua didn't disappoint; the reception was monumental and the noise was thunderous as boats honked their horns, people whistled and shouted, and the steel band played. The excitement was tangible, with maracas being shaken, flags raised and even a prosthetic leg being waved in the air. Seth had managed to gain access to a beautiful yacht berthed across from the quay. It turned out to belong to Pete Townshend of The Who and he kindly agreed to fly one of Row2Recovery's flags from the flagpole. This made a great backdrop for all the photographs and video footage. As 'Legless' approached us, the Antiguan Army was present and lined up along the quay and they did a gun salute when she pulled up alongside.

Emotions were running high and tears of happiness, relief and pride flowed as family members reached forward to touch their loved ones. After the announcement of the final finish time, lots of champagne spraying and more than a few photographs, the crew were allowed to alight from their abode of the past forty-six days. It was not without a few wobbles when three of them set their one foot on solid ground. Skipper Cayle was last off and he managed to quite capably get himself into his wheelchair without a replay of the last time. The Antiguan

Army stood to attention and made a tunnel with their guns for the crew to go through. They were then taken aside for media photographs. Once the photographs were done, Pete Townshend made his way over to congratulate them. From there it was into the Copper and Lumber Hotel for media interviews and a Skype call from none other than Prince Harry. Harry had been on standby and made a point of telling them he had had to wait an hour and a half for them. After a hilarious chat with him, when it came time to sign off, and amid much mirth, Cayle said to Harry, 'You look like you need a tan, mate.'

The next few days saw us consume between us more than a few rum punches, piña coladas and Wadadli beers to cap off our ten sun-filled days on the island. It was time for us to head back to the UK. We were rudely accosted by the bracing weather as we stepped off the plane, although Cayle thoroughly enjoyed the freezing air as he still struggled with being constantly hot.

33. Passport

Bronwyn
Early 2016

After nine years of living in the UK and countless seemingly ridiculous tests that cost more money than I care to mention, Cayle's paperwork was finally submitted for his British Citizenship. On Friday, 12 June 2015, the funds were cleared through his bank account. We had hoped this was confirmation that in principle, he had been approved as a citizen.

Unfortunately that was not to be. Glitches meant that Cayle's application was rejected, and not just once. When he left the country in November 2015 to commence the Atlantic Challenge for the second time, he still did not have his British passport. Thankfully, when he returned home from Antigua in January 2016, there was some good news awaiting him in the form of a letter of confirmation.

One step closer to British Nationality, Cayle went to Exeter on 31 March for his citizenship ceremony. He was one of about forty-five people that day, and normal procedure is that the ceremony is only celebrated by a round of applause after all the participants have been sworn in. However, after Cayle had sworn his oath, the mayor of Exeter made an announcement about Cayle and what he had achieved, and with that the room erupted in applause. Cayle was then invited to have his photograph taken with the mayor.

The passport interview on 3 May was successful, and a week later Cayle finally received his British passport. After all these years he could now travel freely without having to get permission and a NATO travel order to do so. What a relief it was, and it came not a moment too soon as his medical discharge date from the military of 15 July 2016 was looming. His Ancestral Visa had expired in 2011, but as long as he was still serving in the British Military he was allowed to remain in the country. If he had not been issued with his British passport before being discharged, he would have had to return to South Africa and all his benefits would have fallen away – the alternative future this presented doesn't bear thinking about.

While the courier was still reversing away from the house, the precious envelope was ripped open and Cayle was online with his hot-off-the-press British passport in his hand, booking a trip to Iceland.

34. Royals

It was towards the end of June 2012, when Cayle was still in QEHB and only a few days out of his coma, that we had our first encounter with the British royal family. There had been a lot of activity around Ward 412 with people scurrying backwards and forwards, furniture being moved, light bulbs changed and everything in sight being polished in anticipation of a VIP.

Although out of visiting hours, we were allowed to sit at Cayle's bedside and wait with him. Moments later, totally unannounced, in walked the then Prince Charles. At 5ft 10in he is shorter than I expected, but certainly has a presence about him. On entering the ward, he chatted with Bryan and his mum for a few minutes and had a laugh with them. He then walked across the ward to us, shook hands with each of us and chatted for a few minutes; the conversation flowed easily. He sat down on the chair beside Cayle's bed and they spoke for quite some time. He has very blue eyes, which I had not previously noticed, and he really listened and made a lot of eye contact with Cayle. It was interesting to note that Cayle did not seem to be at all intimidated by him; he could have been speaking to his next-door neighbour. Just as Prince Charles was about to leave us, I cheekily asked if he'd make an entry in Cayle's patient's diary, which he agreed to do but told us that he has awful handwriting and most probably none of us would be able to read it. I offered him my pen, which he politely declined, instead taking out of his suit jacket pocket a beautiful fountain pen. He wrote Cayle this message:

It was marvellous to see you during my visit and I do hope you will soon make a speedy recovery. This brings you my kindest and most heartening wishes. Charles.

With that, Prince Charles stood up, shook our hands again and walked away. It all felt totally surreal.

* * *

Just over a year after meeting Prince Charles, in 2013 Cayle and I were invited by SSAFA to meet the Queen and Prince Philip for the opening of SSAFA's new head office in London. Cayle had been staying at Norton House a few days prior and he had been chatting to Mike. Mike had been at SSAFA head office for a briefing about the Queen's visit and he was pleased to tell Cayle that there would be approximately 100 of us present and that we had been divided into four groups – one for each of the royals attending – the Queen, Prince Philip, the Prince and Princess Michael of Kent. Cayle and I had been placed in the group to meet the Queen. Delighted and honoured to hear this, Cayle expressed his desire to meet Prince Philip as well … so Mike made a call.

In the run-up to the big day, I had been diligently practising my curtsy and frantically trying to remember that it's 'ma'am' like jam'. We were given instructions to be at the venue by no later than 10.30 as the lifts would be closed for security reasons. The moment we entered the premises, Cayle was approached by the media asking if he would be prepared to be interviewed after the event. It was at this point that we were informed that, as requested, Cayle would be able to meet Prince Philip as well.

'Well, that's a win!' He beamed at me.

Promptly at 11.15 the Queen and the Duke of Edinburgh were escorted to the entrance of the building. It was not long before, almost by magic and completely by surprise, the Queen stood in front of us. Cayle was introduced to her but she already knew exactly who he was.

'Do I understand you are going to be doing something idiotic?' she said.

'Yes, Ma'am, I'm going to be rowing across the Atlantic. I leave in a week's time for the Canary Islands and we set out on about the second of December,' he replied.

'Is this a good time to go?' she continued.

'It's out of hurricane season, so probably the best time to do it.'

'Oh, that's good,' she said, with a little chuckle.

Moments later, she turned to me and I was so flustered with the reality that I was about to shake the Queen's hand that I forgot what to say, and I think I may even have said 'hello' instead of my practised 'ma'am'. She graciously smiled at me as I attempted to do some form of wobbly curtsy, which I am sure would have been enough to embarrass my dear old grandmother.

The Queen then asked how SSAFA had helped me and I was able to tell her that we had stayed on and off at Norton House since Cayle was injured and that they had been the most incredible support to us.

Moving on to speak to Mike who was standing next to me, as they engaged in conversation, Cayle and I were led away to the back of the line of people in another room where Prince Philip was greeting people.

Cayle was hoping for a famously inappropriate Prince Philip gaffe – and he did not disappoint. He too knew about Cayle and the upcoming row and they chatted briefly about it before he pointed to Cayle's prosthetics and said, 'You should get them to put wheels on those – you'll be able to get around much easier!'

We all roared with laughter and as the Duke walked away, Cayle looked at me, with a massive grin on his face, and said, 'I love him!'

An hour after commencing, the event was over. The Queen turned to Prince Philip as she walked past Cayle and said, 'Do you know what this young man is going to be doing?'

To which the Duke responded, 'Yes – the boy's nuts!'

And with that they were gone. What a memorable day.

We had no idea the fluster Prince Philip's joke would cause worldwide in the media. I think Cayle appeared in every single newspaper in the UK, as well as on most TV channels here and abroad. The response to Prince Philip's comment to Cayle was very varied and interesting and as Cayle said, 'I hoped for a gaffe and I was not at all offended by it, so no need for anyone to be offended on my behalf.'

Our drive home to Dartmouth was filled with stories of the day and we marvelled at the fact that we had just been in the presence of the Queen and the Duke of Edinburgh.

* * *

On 14 March 2014 Seth and I were invited to a function at the Henley River and Rowing Museum, where we met up with the Row2Recovery crew that Cayle had been a part of in 2013, the previous Row2Recovery crew from 2012, as well as Sir Steve Redgrave and some of the Olympic and Paralympic rowing medallists. Prince Harry was the honorary guest and he presented the R2R rowers with medals for completing the challenge. Seth and I waited at the end of the line as Harry worked his way along and we were honoured to meet him and shake his hand.

After the presentation we went downstairs for a light lunch while Prince Harry mingled with the crowd. He spent a fair amount of time chatting to Cayle, Seth and James Kayll and they teased him about his toe, which he had broken a few weeks before starting the Walking with the Wounded expedition to the South Pole. It had still caused him discomfort on the expedition and he had recently been heard complaining about it on camera. Harry laughed at their ribbing, looking at Cayle as if to say that his toe was nothing compared to what Cayle has to deal with.

He was genuinely interested in the row, so Cayle asked him if he would be prepared to row the Pacific with him and James: without quoting his exact words, his answer was a definite no! He has a wicked sense of humour and we were all completely at ease in his presence.

After lunch, we made our way outside to where a trailer carrying *Endeavour* was parked. Harry was able to have a close look at the boat and ask questions about the crossing. He was very interested in how Cayle and Scott had manoeuvred their way around the vessel during the challenge, and he and Cayle spoke for quite some time about the logistics of it all.

A few hours after arriving, Harry was chauffeured away. On the drive home, I chattered non-stop in the car about what a wonderful day it had been. We didn't know then that Cayle and Harry would cross paths numerous times over the following few years.

* * *

Cayle had a very busy day on 6 November 2014. In the morning he did a motivational talk with James Kayll at BNY Mellon (Bank of New York) in London. From there he went to Buckingham Palace to a reception to thank those involved in the medical care, recovery and rehabilitation of British Servicemen and women while in Afghanistan. Among the 300 guests were other wounded servicemen. Hosting the event were the Queen, Prince William and Prince Harry. When the Queen made her appearance, the other guests moved towards her but Cayle stepped back to allow the people who hadn't met her before to get their chance. The Queen saw him over all the heads and nodded at him in recognition. He felt quite honoured that she seemed to remember him.

A totally different scenario took place when Harry spotted Cayle – he pointed at him and then pushed through the masses. Walking up to Cayle, he smiled and gestured towards Cayle's beard then said, 'Do you mind if I … is it okay if I … ah, never mind, I'm just going to do it anyway …'

And he started stroking Cayle's beard. 'It's amazing and so soft – never shave that off!'

Of course they both started laughing, as did those around them.

* * *

Late at night on Friday, 12 June 2015, Cayle and I were at home watching a DVD and Cayle kept looking down at his phone. Eventually he paused the film and said Captain Harry Amos was trying to get hold of him and that, judging by the number of calls, it was obviously something of importance. Cayle wheeled into the kitchen to return the call and, among laughter and questioning, I heard him sounding very unsure and then, 'Yes, General.'

A few minutes later Cayle wheeled back into the lounge with a stunned look on his face. When I asked what was going on, he said Harry was phoning to congratulate him on his appointment to MBE (Member of the Military Division of the Most Excellent Order of the British Empire) and when he had told Harry that he didn't believe him, Major General Rutherford-Jones had come on the line to confirm it. They had seen it on the government website. Being as humble as he is, and still somewhat shell-shocked, Cayle asked that nothing be made public quite yet. That didn't last long, because within minutes it was posted onto his Facebook page and the well-wishes started pouring in. He was totally overwhelmed by the nomination and the response.

The excitement of Cayle receiving his investiture invitation through the post was immense, mine probably greater than his. There was no doubt that what he held in his hand was from the Queen, and I was hopping up and down next to him like a kid on Christmas Day while he opened it. The date was set for Thursday, 17 September 2015 and we were not yet sure who would be officiating. Seth, who was by now working for Salesforce and based in Ireland, took leave from work to come over, and Richard would be up from Mallorca in Spain.

As it was to be held at Windsor Castle, we organised with Mike to stay at Norton House in Surrey the night before. We were up early to get dressed in our finery and were standing on the driveway outside Norton House when Cayle casually said, 'I even polished my shoes!'

Our natural reaction was to look down and when we did, we saw that his prosthetic feet were gleaming. We all burst out laughing.

Making our way along the motorway to Windsor for the ceremony, we soon spotted the Castle.

'Is the flag flying?' asked Seth in anticipation.

'No flag!' I announced from the back seat.

'Ooooh, so who is going to be officiating then?' wondered Seth.

'Well, I've not met William yet, so it would be cool if it's him,' said Cayle.

As we pulled up at the front gate, the guard asked for our invitations to validate us. He then mentioned that it was indeed Prince William who would be officiating.

From the gate guard to the ushers and everyone in between, each person was genuine with their congratulations and interest in Cayle. We were guided towards the entrance, where we made our way to the reception area to remove our coats before climbing a beautiful staircase, separating on the landing at the top as Cayle was taken aside and ushered to where he was to wait, and we were shown to our seats. I couldn't help glancing around the massive, spectacularly adorned room and marvelling at how this little South African farm boy had found his way to Windsor Castle, receiving such recognition by royalty. It felt removed from reality.

Before the proceedings, the audience had been told that clapping was not permitted during the ceremony. With programme in hand, I knew how far down the list Cayle was and as the person before him walked towards Prince William, I couldn't help myself and I bobbed up and down in my seat, fascinator wobbling on my head, punching the air and whispering a little too loudly, 'That's my boy, that's my boy!' as I saw Cayle making his way across the room from the left.

'Mom, shhh,' said Seth, laughing at me.

Nervously, Cayle stopped in front of William, briefly bowed his head and shook William's hand. Then, from a distance, we noticed Cayle taking a couple of small steps away from William, then a couple of small steps forwards, then a couple more backwards, and then forwards again and then he stood still. We could hear a few giggles coming from the front row but, without the use of microphones, we couldn't hear what was being said. Cayle stood with his back to us chatting to Prince William for quite a few minutes before shaking his hand again and then turning right and walking out of the room, leaving us wondering what his soft shoe shuffle had been about.

When we met up with Cayle in the foyer after the ceremony, he told us that when he came to take his place in front of William, the pile of the carpet was so thick that he was struggling to stand still on his prosthetic legs. Seeing Cayle had a problem, William had leaned forward to ask him if he was okay, to which Cayle responded, 'No, your carpet's fucking me up.'

Thankfully Prince William had laughed before offering his left arm for Cayle to hold onto to steady himself. William had asked Cayle about the 2013 Atlantic Row and the upcoming one, and he wished him the best of luck. Cayle was presented with his MBE medal and then it was over – except that he now has three letters after his name.

To this day, Cayle still has no idea who nominated him for the MBE.

35. Television

Bronwyn
Late 2015

It was to be the first time I had been on national television, but it certainly wasn't the first time for Cayle.

Back in September 2015 I had received a phone call from Cayle's PRO (Personnel Recovery Officer) regarding surprising Cayle for ITV's *Surprise Surprise* Christmas edition. I would never dare put Cayle's name forward for anything like this, mainly because he doesn't believe he deserves the recognition. Lieutenant Colonel Ian Thomas believed otherwise and so I received a call from Ollie Knowles, a researcher for ITV, to get a bit of Cayle's story and to let me know how things would proceed.

Cayle is one of the most observant people I know and it was really hard keeping the surprise from him, but all the subterfuge paid off. Cayle and I initially had an informal online interview under the pretence that ITV were looking at doing a documentary on 'Overcoming Adversity'. We then arranged for a producer and full four-man crew to come to spend a day filming with me at home on Monday, 19 October. Thankfully, it would be while Cayle was competing in the Icarus Trophy and he would be in the air somewhere over the West Coast of America, so it was easy for me to get things ready without him being aware.

At 8.30 am, two big black vans pulled up outside the house and our home was soon bustling with activity as the big set-up began. The producer gave directions as four crew, including Ollie, bustled around setting things up. Christmas music was requested to make it even more festive and I was happy to oblige using my laptop. It was incredible to watch the house being transformed into a Christmas wonderland, as the crew had brought everything from a tree, to the decorations, and even Christmas presents. While they were decorating and setting up, I was asked to dig out a few photographs of Cayle's life over the years. The photos would be used throughout the show. I pulled a large box of memories out of the cupboard; I hadn't realised how difficult looking back would be. So many happy times when the boys were growing up, both of them always so active even from an early age. The producer wanted photographs from when Cayle was a toddler right up to him leaving for Afghanistan, and my reaction while flipping through them astonished me. Who could have known that things would turn out like this? Then I asked myself, who could have known that he would be touching lives the way he was? The old saying 'every cloud has a silver lining' popped into my head.

What a day it turned out to be! I was elated but exhausted when the ITV crew eventually left late that afternoon, and pleased with how things seemed to have gone.

As expected, it had all taken longer than anticipated, so the crew ended up having to race out of the house for another appointment up in London that night. To help them out, I said I was happy to clean up – never for one moment considering how difficult it is to get rid of glitter! It was absolutely everywhere: on the sofa, in the wood grain of the dining table, all over the kitchen, trampled throughout the house, and even on my laptop, which could only have happened when we changed the Christmas music. It remains on the sofa to this day, even though I have vacuumed it countless times.

When Cayle returned home from America at the end of October I had hoped that I had eradicated all traces of ITV's presence, but it didn't take long before he mentioned the dratted glitter. Thankfully I could say that I had conveniently had a birthday while he was away so it must have come off one of my cards – under no circumstances must he find out what had taken place or it would spoil the surprise.

Monday, 9 November was the day of Cayle's surprise. He was under the impression that he and the Row2Recovery crew were away to do boat trials and ITV would be there doing some filming. His crew had only been informed of the real reason the night before so as not to have time to spill the beans to him.

Mid-morning I received a text message from him that simply said 'You dick', followed closely by 'Love you Ma xx'. I realised that he must have had his surprise from rowing legend James Cracknell, at which point I could breathe a sigh of relief knowing that the secret had been kept safe for those two months.

Part of Cayle's surprise was being taken for a flight in a Spitfire and his words immediately after were 'Epic, absolutely epic'. He phoned me that evening to tell me how things had gone and also to let me know that he had eventually been told that it wasn't me who had nominated him for the surprise and that I was therefore off the hook.

On the evening of Friday, 4 December, I was on a train up to London once again. I arrived at Paddington Station and was taken by a driver to a hotel near the ITV studios to be ready for filming the following day. Cayle had flown out to La Gomera in the Canary Islands a few days before to prepare the boat for the second row.

I'd been chatting to Ollie over the previous few weeks and he had mentioned that I'd be able to have a tour of the studio during the day before filming took place in the evening, and I was very excited about that. On the morning of filming, I was met in the hotel lobby by Ollie and his assistant and they informed me of the day's procedures and the timings. There seemed to be a fair number of phone calls and messaging going on and I put this down to the organisation involved in a TV show of that scale. I was then handed a loose script to read through, but noticed that the front and back pages had been torn. They told me that it was because I was not allowed to know anything about the other participants in the programme. I was advised to go back up to my hotel room to wait for hair and make-up to come to me in the afternoon.

Lying down on the hotel bed, I took my phone out of my pocket and had a quick look at Facebook. There was a photograph of Cayle in La Gomera with the caption: 'Cayle working the media like a pro this morning.'

I presume it was nerves (even though I had taken a few natural anxiety tablets) that made me babble away throughout my entire three-hour makeover. Once ready, I was collected from the hotel and driven to the ITV studios. On arrival, I was given instructions to wait at the front door for Ollie to take me into the building. He appeared moments later and, after lots of mumbling into headphones, I was whisked down the corridor and directly into a dressing room, where I was left on my own, swinging around on a swivel chair for the better part of an hour. I idly wondered when I was going to be getting my studio tour.

The tour never happened. The dressing room door swung open and before I knew it I was being escorted by Ollie, clutching my hand tightly, to find myself standing directly behind the enormous stage doors. I tried not to think about the potentially millions of people who would watch the programme and for a brief moment panicked that I couldn't go through with it – but it was too late.

The doors opened and there stood Holly Willoughby; I knew there was no turning back. The audience cheered as I walked towards her and she instantly made me feel quite at ease. Hugging me, she said, 'Hello, Bronwyn. Welcome. You look beautiful!' I instantly blushed.

We made our way to the end of the stage and sat on the plush red sofas to chat. I introduced myself and explained why I was there, a little bit about Cayle, about him being injured, and that he was currently in La Gomera waiting to row the Atlantic Ocean for the second time. We then watched footage of the recording I had done in our home, followed by a snippet of the footage from Shorty's helmet camera of Cayle in Afghanistan on 2 May 2012.

Lieutenant Colonel Ian Thomas, who had nominated Cayle for the show, gave the following tribute on-screen:

As a serviceman, Cayle was inspirational, the best in the brigade. He's a great leader and he's somebody that individuals will want to follow. When you meet someone like Cayle, you see what he's gone through and then you see what he's done to make the most of his life; you can't help but realise that this man is a true hero. He's modest, he's determined, but overall he's a real gentleman, an inspiration to be around.

I sat on the red sofa beaming with immense pride at seeing my son in action on the screen, holding a little lilac-ribboned box (which I assumed could only be for me). He and the box were transported in a helicopter, then in the sidecar of a motorbike, then speeding down the River Thames in the actual boat used in a James Bond film, then marching down London's South Bank with the band of the Welsh Guards behind him – still holding the box. I presumed that the box was now with someone else, ready to give to me, but what I didn't know was that Cayle had been flown back from La Gomera, ready to surprise me in turn. When the stage doors opened and the Welsh Guards band marched towards us, nobody was more stunned than me to see Cayle appear among them. In my mind he was busy with preparations in La Gomera; after all, I had seen a photograph of him just that morning, 'chatting to the media' – in actual fact he had been filming the march down the riverside. Working the media like a pro indeed!

It was then that it all made sense as to why my script had been torn and why I had been kept in my hotel room all day and then speedily escorted to the dressing room without my studio tour. It was all worth it when he strode onto that stage, lilac-ribboned box in hand, and I could hardly believe my eyes. I jumped up and went to him, giving him one of the biggest hugs I've ever given him, before we joined Holly back on the sofa.

He and Holly exchanged a few words before Cayle handed me the box, saying, 'I've travelled a long way to deliver this, but this is just a very small something to say I love you very much; I'm incredibly proud of you for putting up with me and this little locket is for you to keep a picture of Seth and I close for the times that we are separated so that we are always with you.'

Inside that little lilac-ribboned box I found a beautiful silver heart locket, which I knew I would treasure forever.

We turned back to Holly and she began, 'Cayle, why has rowing become so much of your rehabilitation?'

'It turned out that rowing was such a great way to test my endurance and to really get out there and experience it,' he said. 'Obviously running is not my strong point these days, but I can go and challenge myself in these other environments and rowing was it, and I absolutely loved it, so I'm looking forward to getting back out to sea again.'

Holly then went on to announce that, on Cayle's behalf, four specially adapted rowing machines would be donated to one of the main rowing centres for injured soldiers.

In the green room after the show, Ollie introduced me to the group of people who had worked tirelessly in the background to make it all possible. I also finally got to meet Lieutenant Colonel Ian Thomas, who had nominated Cayle, and we chuckled about the trouble I had got into when Cayle thought I was behind it all.

This had been one of the most exhilarating days of my life. Cayle and I had a good laugh afterwards about all the secrecy surrounding the show. But, after a quick thirty-six hours in the country, Cayle had to head back out to La Gomera to continue boat preparations with his crew, while I travelled back to Devon with a shiny silver heart locket hanging around my neck; quite different to the dog tags I had worn back in QEHB.

The show was aired on British television on 26 December 2015. I watched it in France while on a skiing holiday with my family; meanwhile Cayle was rowing his way across the Atlantic Ocean for the second time.

36. House

Bronwyn
July 2016

On 14 July 2016, almost ten years to the day after Cayle had passed his army selection, he was medically discharged from the British Army. Given the choice, he said he would genuinely do it all over again – 'minus the oversized party popper, of course'. He considers it an honour to have served.

Once the medical discharge date had been set, Cayle knew that he would have to move out of the military house he had been fortunate enough to have lived in for the past three years. Thus began the search for him to find his own property, and what a search that turned out to be. After many months of frustration at not being able to find anything suitable, mixed with huge disappointment when offers fell through, he finally found a barn conversion on the outskirts of Dartmouth.

On a rainy day in February 2017, he took possession of the property. Richard, at that stage living in France, drove over to lend a hand and he was invaluable in moving furniture and setting up Cayle's workshop for him, making sure that he would be comfortable. Plastic crates containing anything from crockery and cutlery, to camping gear, and enough navigational equipment to prevent any number of people from ever getting lost, were strewn all over Cayle's lounge floor. Slowly and methodically we sorted out what to put where and the cupboards began to bulge.

One evening while Richard was sorting out some electrical issue or other, Cayle was sitting on the floor beside an open crate lifting out items one at a time and making little piles based on relevance. I plonked down next to him to see if I could help and within moments my ears pricked up at an almost-forgotten sound and I was transported back to

QEHB. Cayle had picked up his dog tags and the sound of the discs jangling together on the chain had caused my stomach to lurch and I had a flash-back to those first few days after he had been injured. I had worn those tags every day until he was discharged from the hospital and the noise they made had woven itself into my experience of the place.

That night, as I climbed into bed, my thoughts drifted back to the torrid time we went through, not knowing whether Cayle was going to survive his horrific injuries. Almost five years later, he had moved into his own house and was completely independent.

The military did what they promised and seventeen months after moving in, Cayle was transferred back to the officers' quarters while adaptations began on his own house. Walls were removed for easy wheelchair access, bathrooms altered and exterior paving extended. Underfloor heating and a new kitchen were fitted and the entire interior repainted. All in all it took fourteen months for the works to be completed and he was finally able to move back into his home in September 2019. He settled in quickly.

This house has given him a great base to work from – I'm under no illusion, however, that this means he will be sitting still for too long!

37. Coping

Bronwyn

Writing this book has meant moving myself far out of my comfort zone, overcoming my fears and making myself vulnerable. From the moment I heard about Cayle's injuries I kept a diary of our days in the hospital, in the hardback notebook that Rich bought me while we waited for Cayle to arrive at QEHB, though it was never originally my intention to turn the updates into a book.

Encouraged by hearing countless stories of how this tragedy has affected people's lives, drawing them to hold us in their thoughts and prayers, I came to realise that I had to put it all down on paper. So began my quest to share the story of how our family has been affected by what I can only describe as our worst nightmare. I knew that once I started writing it would be cathartic for me and there would be loads of positives to be taken from it.

I thought back over the number of people who have crossed my path since 2 May 2012, and realised that I have made some lifelong friends. The extraordinary story of my son's refusal to die before his time, his remarkable recovery and rehabilitation, and his subsequent positive outlook on life needed to be shared, and this propelled me forward. My hope is that our story might reach out and touch the life of at least one person who needs it. I just hope that I have done it justice.

I often get asked how I cope. I find that quite an intriguing question and I am never sure if my answer is quite what people expect. How do I cope? I always want to reply to this with, 'What, may I ask, are my options?' I could give up and fall out of life, but what good would that do Cayle or Seth? Or, in fact, me? I have to 'cope'.

I have moments of incredible grief, where my heart still wants to break at what befell us. It seems so unfair that this has happened to my family but, equally, I ask myself 'why not us?' Why do we humans always think it will never happen to us? I think about Cayle's attitude, which is one of 'it's done so let's just move on'. I am constantly amazed at his apparent total acceptance of his situation. Me falling apart or wailing at the injustice is not going to change a thing, but a positive mental attitude and outlook could make a massive difference in someone else's life.

Cayle is an inspiration to so many people and he has got to this place with the unfailing support of family, many friends, but most of all Seth. Seth has remained strong and focused throughout. I am not sure if it was the Royal Marine training or if this has always been his way, highlighted by Cayle's incident. Seth has been my rock when I've felt I'm floundering, straight-talking when I need it, yet compassionate at the same time. He and Cayle are closer than ever as brothers, although Seth does not in any way handle him with kid gloves.

As a person, Cayle has not changed at all. He remains generous, caring, considerate, humble, friendly, funny and loyal, but also as stubborn, moody and fiercely independent as ever he was. He has a way of putting people at ease in his company. Many times someone has inadvertently made a comment about pulling his leg or standing on his toe and have been absolutely mortified about it, but he just laughs and tells them not to stress. Humour and fortitude have been his constant companions.

There have been so many high points on this journey – and there were bound to be some lows. My thoughts drift back to when I had come over to see Cayle in the UK back in 2005, before he and I going travelling together. I realised then that he was no longer a teenager but very much an adult and that it was time to let go and allow him to make his own decisions.

Cayle's incident in 2012 meant that we would be living under the same roof again for a few years and, as Cayle became more independent, we certainly had some moments. I battle to control my mothering instinct, especially when I see he is suffering – be that from having another medical procedure or, more regularly, the problem of his left stump splitting open, or the powerful phantom pains he still has, which cause him to sweat profusely from the agonising discomfort. He has compared the pains to someone hammering a railroad spike into the back of his leg every ten to twenty seconds. And don't even get me started on the insensitive responses of some people towards him, which frequently make me want to lash out at them.

My reactions are out of concern for him, but he quite often feels that I am being overprotective. His preference to be completely self-reliant is so entrenched that he has expressed irritation at me even trying to pass him something, saying he could have done it himself. No amount of me telling him that I generally try to anticipate need, no matter who the person is, seems to sink in.

Does this mean that I do not struggle? I would be lying if I said I don't. The magnitude of what occurred that day is constantly with us. How could this have happened to someone as highly trained as he was? Sometimes I just have to look at Cayle's wheelchair and the emotions well up inside me and I choke back the tears. Or I will see his prosthetic legs leaning idle against the wall in the corner of the lounge – he has to have days off of them when the end of his leg has yet again burst open from the pressure of his stump grinding inside the carbon fibre socket. The left stump in particular continues to be a concern. The skin grafts on it are very thin and they have never toughened up, so it is prone to splitting open if he has spent too much time walking. Mostly he doesn't even mention it, but I notice him put his liners on, then his sockets, and then when he stands up to slide his stumps down into the sockets I'll see him wince and know he's in pain. He will try to stay off his legs for a few days to let the wound heal, but it is not always possible. On the days it is not possible, he will get home and slump into his wheelchair with a sigh of relief. When he removes his liners I'll see that the left one is filled with blood. That's when it hits me – this will be his life forever.

There has rarely been a day since the incident that I have not cried. It's mostly when I think of being outdoors and all the things I know Cayle loved to do. If I go for a walk along the coastal path, I will think of him and how much he loved running and how he will never be able to run again, or even take long walks. If I stroll along a cobbled street, I wonder how he would cope if he was with me. When I go to visit someone, I consider the entrance access and if there are stairs. Then I'm mentally considering if they would be wide enough for him to be able to swing his legs to get up or down them. Most of these things would never have even been on my radar pre-incident and, in some strange way, I hope they have made me more considerate when it comes to others.

Cayle has had to undergo numerous surgeries since the incident, the most significant being one to the back of his head. The pressure sore had resulted in a huge bald patch of about 100mm in diameter. The operation involved creating excess skin by inserting two tissue expanders between his skull and his scalp, which were then slowly expanded over a couple of months by injecting fluid into the sacs. Once the surgeon was sure there was enough skin to be able to cut away the dead scalp, Cayle went back under the knife. The surgery was delicate and what was meant to be a two-hour operation ended up being six hours, with Cayle losing a huge amount of blood and needing to have yet another blood transfusion. We'd lost count by then of how many he's had. Those months were some of the hardest because Cayle was conscious throughout. In hindsight, he said that if he had known the amount of pain he would be in, he probably would not have had the procedure.

Almost four years after his incident, in April 2016, I broached with Cayle the idea of him sitting with me to show me the video footage that Shorty had recorded of the incident out in Afghanistan. Cayle was very reluctant for me to watch it as he said it is not what a mother should see, but I persisted as I felt that it was time. So many other people had already seen it as sections of it have been used for various articles done on Cayle, it felt like it was my turn.

He primed me beforehand by reminding me that it is very graphic and said that he didn't want me crying or causing a scene. I promised not to. I went to sit at my desk; he wheeled up next to me and placed his laptop on the table in front of me. He pressed 'play' and I stared at the screen while he explained to me what was happening. We watched from a few minutes before the explosion and, because I had seen the footage right up to the time of the blast, I found myself holding my breath once I heard the explosion, knowing that Shorty would turn his head to look in Cayle's direction and then run towards him. Nothing could prepare me for what I saw. My son, bloodied and gutturally groaning in agony, face-down in the dust in Afghanistan next to an enormous crater. The rest of it was just a blur to me as my eyes instantly filled with tears and I was unable, thankfully, to clearly see Cayle's horrifically injured face when Shorty rolled him over onto his back. It all happened so quickly and the guys were incredible. How they managed to do what they did after what had just taken place I have no idea, but I will forever be indebted to them. I am still astounded that Cayle can watch the footage but I am sure he does so objectively. I hugged Cayle afterwards and thanked him for showing me, then went up to my bedroom. I lay face down on my bed and wept into the duvet, muffling the sounds that came from deep within.

I think of all the incredible opportunities he has been given, from being sponsored to participate in adventures all over the world, to meeting people he probably would never have crossed paths with, had it not been for this turn of fate. He is motivational and inspirational and doors are opening for him all the time.

So much changed on 2 May 2012. It has been an emotional and amazing journey and we have met some incredible people along the way. I will never forget those first few dark days in QEHB after Cayle came out of his coma. He was fraught with anxiety and had absolutely no hope. His life now is a stark, shining contrast to what he thought it would be.

The bond between my sons and myself has always been strong, but this has made it even stronger. From the moment Cayle was injured, Seth took it upon himself to ensure that nobody treated him any differently and he'd constantly pull people up on it if they did. I am no exception and I have often had my knuckles rapped. Cayle's incredible physical strength and monumental strength of character, combined with Seth's sacrifices and unfailing support, has turned a horrific and life-changing incident into something positive with hope on the horizon.

'Build me a son, O Lord, who will be strong enough to know when he is weak, and brave enough to face himself when he is afraid, one who will be proud and unbending in honest defeat, and humble and gentle in victory'

Douglas MacArthur

38. Hope

Cayle

'Hardship often prepares an ordinary person for an extraordinary destiny'

C.S. Lewis

I came around in the hospital, thanks to the medical teams who were
outstanding. And, thanks to my family being there and to friends,
I started to recover, started eating again, and then it was that, kind of –
'what on earth am I going to do now?' I've always lived for the outdoor
lifestyle, for the adventurous lifestyle, and I very much thought that
that side of my life was over. Not because I'd lost interest in it at all –
I still very much wanted to get out and explore, but it was more because
I thought that people would think that I was too much of a liability and
therefore wouldn't want me to go along on these sorts of things.

This turned out to be completely untrue because, within a few
weeks of me waking up, people were already talking about doing daft
stuff. I just didn't think that I would ever be given the opportunities
to do them any more, and very fortunately that was completely wrong.
So I was still invited to do things and to participate in some pretty cool
sports and adventures. It's been an amazingly freeing experience as
I've been able to explore and adventure and continue to do what I'm
passionate about and that is to see remote parts of the world and meet
great people while doing it.

I'm very, very grateful to all the people who still had faith in my
determination to do things rather than my ability to do them, because
my ability is very limited. Because there are people with the right mental
approach and attitudes towards it, they are patient enough to help me

develop systems that work for me to be able to do it independently and it's awesome.

My life changed dramatically on that day in 2012 when I was blown up, but that's what it was – it was a change … it wasn't the end – it's just different now. I have to approach things with a different mindset. I know I'm not the fastest person in the world and I'm certainly not the most dextrous person in the world, but I know that if you're stubborn enough to do something, you can make it work.

I don't know why, I don't know what, and I don't know where it was from, but there was always one overriding thing that was always, always there – throughout all the hallucinations and all the horror and all the nastiness that I was dreaming about; it was there, almost like a soundtrack, and it was 'I'm not going to die, I'm not going to die, I'm not going to die', playing in the background. It was just this background noise the whole way through. I didn't even know what was going on, I didn't know where I was, I didn't know if I was dead, but I kept saying 'I'm not going to die, I'm not going to die, I'm not going to die'. And then to wake up was bizarre – is this real, is this not real?

Then it dawned on me, the reality of the whole thing. It was just the initial misery of 'what happens next? What do I do? Am I confined to a hospital bed for the rest of my life; am I going to be wheelchair-bound; will I walk again?'

My total lack of knowledge of what people in similar situations were doing with the rest of their lives meant that I honestly believed that this was as good as it was going to get and it terrified and saddened me that I would live the rest of my days in a hospital watching the world go by, too weak to do anything for myself and in constant need of care.

It just turned out to be completely false and I've ended up meeting some amazing people and travelling to some incredible places and doing some awesome stuff. You don't need to do ridiculous things like row oceans and fly trikes – if your personal challenge is to go out into the garden and play chess with a friend then, fine, do it. So even if things go so horrifically, life-changingly wrong, there's definitely still hope. I hope that by participating in the number of challenges that I have been so fortunate to be involved in, we can help raise the profile of wounded servicemen and women and show them early on in their recovery that it may be dark and horrible, and you may have extreme lows, but with the right support and mental attitude we can still achieve amazing things. It certainly does not mean the end of a full and active life if that's what you choose to pursue.

The thing that I still struggle with, and struggled with the most initially, is that everybody looks at me all the time; you can never just blend in and be the grey man.

Wherever I go there is a constant refrain of 'What the hell happened there?!' or, 'That man's got robot legs!'

I can never just blend in. I can't be part of the crowd. I can't just casually walk along and not have everybody staring at me. That's a big thing to get your head around.

Having found myself in this situation, I certainly don't feel like I've achieved anything less for it. Because of the kind of people I am very fortunate to be surrounded with, the kind of opportunities I have been able to grasp, the people who I have met and the places I have been to, I absolutely am living a fantastic life. I'm doing all right. There is a life beyond injury.

39. Future

Cayle

Having now been out of the military and rehabilitation for some years, I have settled into my home in Devon, just outside of Dartmouth. I have multiple projects on the go to keep me busy, including fitting out a campervan, which has been an excellent way to relearn workshop skills with fewer fingers than before. The van itself will hopefully offer me a great base of operations for future adventures.

The next big expedition that I am currently working on is a sea-kayaking expedition along The Inside Passage, which runs up the Pacific north-west coastline from just south of Seattle up to Skagway in Alaska. The direct route is around 1,400 nautical miles; however, we expect to be exploring a fair bit along the way, so it will be a bit further than that. It should take us around 100 days to complete. We hoped to depart at the beginning of May 2022 with a team of wounded military veterans, but COVID forced us to defer the trip for a year to May 2023.

This adventure will be done to raise money for military charities. These charities have played an enormous part in my rehab and I feel very strongly about giving back after they have done so much for me. It will hopefully mean that they can continue to support people who find themselves in a similar position to me.

I do not know what the future holds. But I do know that I am extremely fortunate to be surrounded by great people. I am excited to see what sits just around the corner and the adventures it will bring.

'Our lives are not determined by what happens to us, but how we react to what happens; not by what life brings us, but by the attitude we bring to life. A positive attitude causes a chain reaction of positive thoughts, events and outcomes. It is a catalyst, a spark that creates extraordinary results.'

Anonymous

Testimonials

Paddy Nicoll

Cayle is the most extraordinary guy; I rather wished we had served together in the army. It's a testament to his amazing strength of character, his tough South African roots, his kind but resolved nature, and his acute professionalism as a mariner that he was able to captain a crew mostly made up of wounded veterans of higher military rank than himself. This is an often overlooked factor of Cayle's success as a skipper. Military groups, even those made up of veterans, tend to default to previous ranks. Making up Cayle's crew was a serving Royal Marine Colour-Sergeant of twenty-five years of operational experience, which included a tour of Northern Ireland, of Iraq and three of Afghanistan, some of which were on Special Duties. Also in the crew was a Royal Air Force Flight-Sergeant with thousands of hours as a parachute instructor, his students often from the Special Forces. And finally a former Irish Guardsman, a peer also wounded in action in Afghanistan. Cayle had been a relatively junior Lance-Corporal (albeit as a highly respected sharpshooter in the Helmand Brigade Reconnaissance Force), but his crew naturally took to him as their skipper.

Just before I met Cayle, I had no plans to organise a second Atlantic crossing – I'd only just begun Row2Recovery's national adaptive rowing programme for wounded, injured and sick Service personnel, in partnership with British Rowing (the national governing body) and Help for Heroes' Sports Recovery wing. But Rory Mackenzie, who was one of the wounded veterans in our first crew, approached me about being asked by Atlantic Campaigns, the organisers of the Atlantic Rowing Challenge, to put together another team of wounded rowers for the 2012 race.

The first team member we selected was Mark Jenkins, who, as a military physiotherapist, had worked with Rory during his recovery. Then I received an unsolicited offer of help from James Kayll, a recently retired army officer, prompted by my call to arms on social media. A quick check of his Facebook page revealed that he had already rowed the Indian Ocean and had a long history of ocean sailing – thus I found the skipper! The remaining two rowers were proposed by those first two crew members: Scott Blaney by Mark and Cayle by James. This was when I first met the legendary Cayle Royce!

I was initially very worried about including Cayle. His injury had only occurred in May 2012; it seemed far too early for him to undertake such a challenge. Neil Heritage, a double-amputee from our first crew, had already proved to a sceptical medical world that a severely wounded soldier was capable of undertaking such an extreme endeavour as rowing an ocean unsupported. But it is easy to forget how soon after Cayle's wounding in Afghan the row was.

Following the incredible moment in 2014 when the second Row2Recovery boat arrived safely to a massive crowd of well-wishers into Antigua's English Harbour, I certainly had no further ambitions to organise another row. There was a strong feeling among the military charity community that the story had been told. But the elephant in the room, namely that there had always been two able-bodied veterans in each crew, always nagged at me. Finally the itch had to be scratched and unfortunately for Cayle, he was the only person on the planet capable of leading such an endeavour. And so, out of the blue, I wrote an email to him asking if he fancied skippering an all-amputee military Atlantic crew.

It was more than a month later that I finally got my reply. Thankfully I avoided being dragged by James around his salubrious London haunts after an unplanned reunion of the crew. But Cayle hadn't been so fortunate and so the following morning, when I had arranged to meet Cayle and Seth for breakfast, Cayle wasn't in the best state of mind to negotiate. The plan was set. I'll never forget Seth's description that morning of the moment that Cayle had got my email request.

Apparently they had been sitting together catching up on emails, when Cayle suddenly went white, closed his eyes and let out a distraught sigh. Seth said that he'd assumed that Cayle had heard some ghastly news, but Cayle explained the horrific nature of the request. I knew what a massive ask it was – the only extreme rowing plan that Cayle had on the horizon was an attempt on the Pacific Ocean with James; the idea of rowing the Atlantic a second time was the furthest thing from his mind. But true to form, he stepped up to the plate.

Cayle took to the task of skippering his crew with predicted professionalism. In the run-up to the race, not only was he committed to taking part in a paratriking race down the west coast of America, he was booked in for some major and long-running surgery. Despite this, he managed to achieve the purchase of a new boat, including the major logistic challenges that come with equipping it, and get his crew ready.

When ITV chose to devote an entire segment of *Surprise Surprise* to Cayle, the producers asked me if I could think of something that he would like as his treat. As a Trustee of Prince Harry's Endeavour Fund, I had just witnessed an Endeavour beneficiary, Alan Robinson, who had become the first military amputee since Sir Douglas Bader to fly a Spitfire solo, take part in the fly-off of forty spitfires and Hurricanes to celebrate the seventy-fifth anniversary of the Battle of Britain. Knowing that the Spitfire Academy pilots could take passengers in one of their twin-seater Spitfires, I could think of no better treat for Cayle, who was not only a pilot himself but a massive enthusiast of all things military history.

Seth

Cayle was always going to do the first row. I told him he was an idiot for wanting to do it, not because he wasn't capable, but because it sounded like a really shitty thing to do, but I knew he needed to do it. Even if he hadn't been blown up and someone had said 'Do you want to row across the Atlantic Ocean?', he would have said yes and I would have said no.

Nothing that Cayle has done since he was blown up has surprised me. That's not saying it in a negative way, or that he's not achieved enough, because he clearly has, but there are opportunities that would not have presented themselves if he hadn't been blown up. Would he swap everything to have his legs and his hand back? Yes, in fact he'd probably swap all of that just to have his hand back … MBE, rowing, flying. That's pretty hardcore.

Cayle is like the worst older sibling because he's such an overachieving person … cheers dickhead! I can understand why everyone else finds him inspiring and that makes him even more annoying. For me it's just 'there he goes again'. But Cayle won't do anything he's not comfortable with, like running on blades or climbing a mountain. That's not to say that the things he does aren't incredible – they're just different and more suited to the Cayle we know. Given the opportunity, he would have rowed every ocean on the planet before he got 'schwacked'. It's not because he's been blown up that he's become an adventurous person, and that's kind of the essence of it. Cayle was determined to do really stupid shit; now he just does it with half a body.

Growing up, he and I were consistently competitive and I think the reason we started recreational shooting was for the competition. We tried to find something that Cayle and I could compete at on an even level. It's not quite even because once again knees and a hand help massively when it comes to being able to pivot, but it's as close as dammit.

As kids, Cayle had been overly protective of me and I know he still is. I know that he looks out for me. He would always be the 'big brother' in every scenario and now being able to return the favour for him, occasionally, is quite nice.

Richard

I don't know how to put it into words, but I just don't know where Cayle found the strength. When he came out of his coma he was just so determined. The pain he must have been in, the physical experience that he must have had with nothing working properly … everything weak and shaky. Yet he still pushed through and that to me was amazing. I don't know if you quite understand what I am saying – if I get a tummy bug, I'm flat-out. If I cut my nails too short, I complain. Every single part of him was jagged, it was wrecked … breathing, swallowing, eating, shitting, peeing... plus raw-ended stumps. Cayle had massive challenges that he seemed totally unprepared for. I wondered how I could motivate him, what I could do, what I could say to a man who is savagely independent?

I think he is a very special young man. There is no way that this is standard … the way he does what he does. He's exceptional and is certainly a motivation for others, but I doubt many people have the determination he has. If he hadn't been that super fit he'd be dead, no doubt; there's no way he could take that hammering in the hospital and come out unscarred. He just refused to give up. There was nothing left of him when he came out – he'd used it all up, he certainly fought.

I think he looked the worst when Prince Charles visited, and then when we went to the airshow. We felt it was necessary to get him out in public, but the reaction of people was unexpected and it just broke my heart. It was hard to imagine that he would improve from that. I thought that that was where he was going to remain, that would be Cayle's life now … a shell of his former self. I'm amazed that he turned it around and this is where he is. His attitude was, 'I am not going to spend any time in my wheelchair'. A couple of times I made the mistake of mentally trying to put myself in his position, but it was just too hard.

He must have felt like death after all the drugs and the pain and not knowing what the future was going to hold. What spark kept him going; what turned him around?

We had a terrible incident when we went to Tedworth House. We were all there and we talked Cayle into riding on one of those Segway things. He got on it and obviously it isn't designed for a shorter person … you have to have feet, and inevitably he fell off, and as it fell forward he also fell forward. The bar of the Segway smashed his hand and his stumps went straight into the concrete. It was those sort of days that I just felt so utterly devastated … I felt that he would never ever be able to do anything … better he just stay in his wheelchair, but no, he was ashen and he was shaken, but it was only half an hour and he was back in his chair and doing stuff. Those are the moments that I remember. The incredible 'bounce-back', Cayle's amazing strength in those times. Where does that strength come from? I guess his attitude was 'what else can you do?' The sun comes up and you get out of bed.

Andrew Stewart

An email from Major General Stewart on the announcement of Cayle's MBE

Dear Bronwyn,

What fantastic news it is to hear that Cayle has been made a Member of the British Empire. I honestly cannot think of a more deserving person to be recognised in such a way. He is an example to everyone of how to overcome life changing injuries and he should be immensely proud of what he has achieved.

Back in May 2012 it was impossible to believe that he would achieve what he has, but I do remember you telling him that while his life had changed, new opportunities would arise. You were so right, but the fact he has seized those opportunities comes down to his determination and your support. I hope that you will feel quietly proud of your part in his recovery and that a little part of that MBE is yours. If you do not, you should.

With all my very best wishes and congratulations.

Yours sincerely
Andrew

Gus Fair

Excerpts from a handwritten letter from Brigadier AGC Fair DSO (Distinguished Service Order), The Light Dragoons, Swanton Morley, Norfolk after a visit to Cayle in QEHB

Dear Roycey

I was relieved to find that you retain that same strength of character and spirit that I knew you for from my time at RD [Regimental Duties]. However devastated you are about the loss of your legs you should recognise that it was never your legs that set you apart from others, they did not define you. It was your character and spirit that did those things.

So just as your legs in themselves did not define you previously, the absence of them should not in itself define you going forward. You evidently remain a determined fighter and an impressive individual with a different but no less bright future ahead of you. However, to realise your potential and to exploit the opportunities of your new life you must first mentally adjust and get yourself physically fit.

Selection is designed to push individuals into mental and physical lows, to challenge their determination and inner strength. You now face the challenges of recovery and rehabilitation which will bring mental and physical highs and lows. Just as I was confident that you would have got through Selection, I am confident that you will find the focus and discipline to successfully come out the other end of rehab and realise your great potential.

In order to find the focus you will need for your recovery and rehab, you will need to park your inevitable concerns regarding your longer term future. You should shelve the long-term questions and planning for now, confident in the immense potential you have and the bright future that lies ahead of you.

Approach the next phase exactly as you would have done Selection; a single-minded focus on getting yourself physically and mentally fit again. Once you are through that hurdle you can switch your efforts back to planning and pursuing your longer-term future.

I do appreciate that all these words may seem trite from someone who can have little understanding of the situation in which you find yourself now. What I have written here is genuine and I hope it helps a little.

Yours sincerely
Gus

Captain Harry Amos

Learning to become a reconnaissance soldier is not just hard work; the role demands a natural aptitude that requires intelligence and imagination, and an eye for detail. There is the critical ability to communicate complex and dangerous situations quickly, by day or night and in all theatres of war, up the chain of command to inform the formations behind you of what is to come. We are often communicating from small cold ditches in the ground, atop of wet grassy knolls, or from behind hot rocky outcrops, almost always in austere, uncomfortable conditions and, of course, way behind enemy lines. In Afghanistan our role is less covert. Instead of quietly inserting beyond the forward line of our own troops, we instead use the tactic 'Recce by Fire' as we aim to find, feel and understand the civilian territories occupied by the Taliban (or worse). Operations are much more kinetic but equally as nuanced. You've got to remain cool and instead of using a fire fight as an excuse to assault, we use it as an opportunity to understand the enemy's strengths, dispositions, positions and modus operandi as we absorb the fire. This is much more useful to our bosses in Brigade HQ than just killing a Taliban sniper team. Of course, as much as we could, we also used our special access to high-level intelligence and strike capability to destroy strategic Taliban command nodes, IED factories and weapons caches. This is what we were doing the day Roycey was hit.

Cayle is inbuilt with that natural guile, fitness, and a fantastic sense of humour (that improves more and more as situations deteriorate), which meant he was perfectly placed in the selected Brigade Reconnaissance Force and in my troop. There's a standout trait that came with Cayle; it was that gritty resilience, there long before he joined the army I'm sure, and there without any training or nurturing from me. The saying 'when the going gets tough, the tough get going' was made for Roycey.

With Roycey you have a guy who you have to hold back as opposed to drive forward. Most men you have to drive hard to get them to move towards danger, but some, only a handful, are chomping at the bit to get into the action. One has to keep them on the leash so they don't overextend, but they are always ready to go hard and fast into the fray when needed. I much preferred that kind of soldier. I remember seeing Cayle operate for the first time and thought 'this guy is worth his salt'.

From my experience, South Africans often come with that dry sense of humour well suited to soldiering. There's also this sense of personal pride and professionalism that meant that the bare minimum was never enough. This is Roycey all over. Added to that was his intellect, which meant that not only did I have a guy who could get down and dirty, I had a guy who could think and do the more complicated, nuanced tasks as well. Troopers love to complain and rarely volunteer to do the hard stuff but in the BRF we were looking for people who would put their hand up – Roycey always did. Once on a recce exercise in Alberta, on the Canadian plains, Roycey and I laid on the side of a roasting mosquito strewn hill for days looking down on a pretend petrol station manned by mannequins. He had volunteered for the job over the much more comfortable option of the Troop hide behind the hill. There was not one complaint from him – just his dry cheerfulness for hours on end. He was the ace in my pack of cards, the most talented trooper in my Troop and the one guy I never had to worry about.

As a Troop Leader one is looking to foster the next generation of junior leaders; Roycey is a natural and he had already made an impression with the senior echelons of the squadron as well. He was able to do this without stepping on anyone else and you could see that people around him, his colleagues and his friends, would naturally defer to him. He took the mantle and, as far as I ever saw, he sought to live up to the respect that people had for him. He was a natural director and his attitude and presence were reassuring to the team around him, making him a vital part of the fabric of the troop. You could go as far as to say that I modelled the troop on Roycey. If there was ever a tough recce task that needed a trustworthy, independent, bright guy, I'd gladly send him. Roycey was the top guy for that kind of stuff and he loved it. He was a linchpin holding his team together and leading by example.

Troops and Sections (with the Troops) are designed so that they are able to take a casualty and remain functional. Everybody is trained to be multi-skilled and can do everyone else's job if needs be. Each soldier is able and responsible to fill the gap of an injured teammate when necessary. I was confident that if ever I wasn't there, the troop would be able to operate at maximum ability and utterly professionally because the team was made up of people like Cayle and Shorty. We were in a really good place and I could trust these guys.

When Roycey was hit, people had to step up, and they did. It's remarkable to see and no one hesitated from the moment the IED went off. The situation was terrifying but the guys did what needed to be done. Jacko, the medic, launched into action and applied the tourniquets critical to keeping Roycey alive within seconds. Shorty, who had been blown off his feet by the explosion, continued to lead his section and secured the site around Roycey. Lads like Matty Appleby, one of his junior guys, jumped in as point man in Roycey's stead. The guys cleared the HLS with Valons [mine detectors], all while we coordinated Tiger Gunships to suppress Taliban small arms fire and the Chinook Medical Emergency Response Team [MERT] to fly in on a hot landing zone. In twenty-two minutes Cayle was on the helicopter heading back to Bastion, 80km away.

The war didn't stop when Cayle was injured and the troop went out two days later on another Heli assault. That op was hard, really really hard, and aside from the fact that we were missing our best trooper, I can tell you that the guys were absolutely bricking it. I have never been so afraid in my life and not just for my guys but for myself … I was looking at the ground as if it was going to fucking eat my legs… and then the shooting started and we were back at it. Everybody was hurting but we had to re-cock and get out there again, and we did, but it wasn't the same without him, and while we could continue to do the job, there was a massive void left by Roycey. Cayle was a key team member… really, really key. I looked up to him, the guys around him looked up to him. He was one of the drivers driving the train forward in the day-to-day. That was where he stood in the troop.

Towards the end of the tour, my challenge as the Troop leader was to hold guys back so not to push our luck or overextend, which was a great problem to have. The fear generated from Roycey's incident, and other incidents including Barry (the Troop Sergeant), who lost (and survived) a hand grenade battle, and Corporal Caswell, who was shot through the arm, quickly wore off and we were back to being a bunch of dogs on heat who really wanted to take the fight to the Taliban.

Roycey is just exceptional, he always has been, and so it shouldn't surprise us that he has made such an incredible and unique recovery because he is like that. I talk about him all the time to my friends and my family and to people I've only just met because I'm so unbelievably proud to know him. From ski racing with him in the Swiss Alps, to patrolling across the Kenyan Savannah, to night-time raids in Afghanistan, he has always been the guy to do amazing things, to be active, and to test himself. Most people aren't like that, not like him; people don't just get into boats months after they get blown up and row the Atlantic … and then take up flying with Paramotors (normally requiring two legs) and then row the ocean again; that's not normal. I think he might have become even more fearless since his injuries. But when you've lost as much as he has, I think you then have 'carte blanche' to lead your already exciting life to an even fuller extent than you ever did before because you appreciate life so much more. I certainly wish that for Roycey.

David Rutherford-Jones

Letter from Major General David Rutherford-Jones CB, Colonel The Light Dragoons after the second Atlantic Row

4 February 2016
Dear Bronwyn and Cayle,

A new World achievement, truly on a global scale. Incredible.

We Light Dragoons, all of us and our families too, are incredibly proud of you Cayle, and of course your team. But we are of course especially proud of you personally, our Light Dragoon. And Bronwyn, we are in awe of you too; how proud you must feel. It seems to me team Royce is frankly formidable, and very long indeed on personal stocks of resilience, courage, humour and determination.

I think there is a true quality around the inspiration and humility borne out of the expeditions that you have completed Cayle, since you recovered. They are on one level extraordinary feats of human conquest, and on another a deeply human story of a singular determination not to be beaten. The example you have set for so many people, not simply those who like you are physically changed, but many many others who just struggle in life to get somewhere, is frankly immeasurable.

I say, Celebrate, Celebrate, Celebrate. Return to the UK safely. We look forward to seeing you on your return.

Your Light Dragoon family salutes you.

Best wishes,
David RJ

Jamie Phillips

When we moved into the military accommodation in Dartmouth back in May 2013, our neighbour was an amazing Royal Navy doctor by the name of Jamie Phillips, who was working at the Britannia Royal Naval College in Dartmouth at the time. We became friends with Jamie and his family, and even though they have since left the country, we remain in contact with them. Jamie took a keen interest in Cayle and his injuries and subsequently all his achievements, and he continues to follow his adventures.

In October 2015, Jamie was presenting on 'The Realities of War – Good Medicine in Bad Places' at the World Extreme Medicine Expo in Westminster London and he sent me this:

I used Cayle as an example of what can be achieved if you combine cutting-edge medicine with a remarkably motivated and irrepressible human being. More importantly, I used Cayle as the answer to my question 'What's my why?'

My 'why', why I provide Battlefield Medicine, is that it allows me to give patients like Cayle a second chance at life and to go on to touch the lives of so many other people around them and inspire them to fulfil their potential. I was presenting alongside some remarkable people (Sir Ranulph Fiennes, an astronaut, Polar explorers, etc.). Their stories paled into insignificance against Cayle's story. I was trying to think of a way to finish my talk and exemplify what humans can achieve if motivated and supported. I then showed Cayle's video from the 2013 Atlantic Row and said 'this is my why'.

Monty Halls

Following on from Cayle's first Atlantic row, an article was written for the Land Rover magazine titled 'Tomorrow's Pioneers by Today's Pioneers: Six people who've changed our world nominate the people who they think will change our future'. Monty Halls, TV broadcaster, explorer and marine biologist, nominated Cayle and these are his words:

We have many 'icons' in the modern world, and it seems to me that it's a word that is bandied about somewhat casually in the media today. I was very lucky indeed to work for Nelson Mandela in South Africa during the seminal years of 1993–94 and he remains one of the dominant figures in my life.

Today, however, there is a new brand of hero emerging from the smoke and dust of Afghanistan. It is that of the wounded serviceman, and one who inspires me is a young man called Cayle Royce, who comes from my home town of Dartmouth. A double amputee, he has squared his shoulders at life, rowed the Atlantic, and is a star of exploration of the future.

Lee Spencer

I was injured on 6 January 2014 in a road accident, and after seven weeks in hospital and a month in Hasler Company in Plymouth, I went to Headley Court. When I got to Headley Court, I had no leg, I was in a wheelchair and I was still quite bewildered by everything and trying to make sense of what my new life was going to be from then on. I was in the bed opposite Cayle, who had just come back from rowing the Atlantic the first time, so seeing Cayle and hearing him talking about doing something as extraordinary as rowing across the Atlantic enabled me to actually put in for things and volunteer for things myself that I wouldn't have thought were possible. Cayle absolutely inspired me and this row, which I wouldn't have put in for if it wasn't for Cayle, was going to change my life. It was going to be a defining part of who I'm going to be for the rest of my life.

What I will take away from the row regarding Cayle and me is the fact that we talked and laughed the whole way across. Not one angry word, no arguments, nothing. About a third of the way in when we were losing our auto helms and had to go down to hand steering, three of us advocated that we go onto para-anchor because we just couldn't do what we needed to do. Specifically we couldn't do what Cayle was doing because we couldn't swap – every time we tried to swap someone else onto the hand-steering position, the boat would go into irons (the trapped condition when the bow is headed into the wind and the boat has stalled and is unable to manoeuvre, leaving it at the mercy of the sea and in danger of capsizing) and we'd spend half an hour trying to dig it out. It was a real, real hard and testing period and Cayle did fourteen hours straight hand steering, which utterly dwarfed my eight hours and forty minutes rowing. It's far harder to hand steer – the levels of concentration are just horrific … how he did it I still don't know.

Calum

One of the most uplifting emails I received in response to my updates when Cayle was in QEHB was this from a school friend of Cayle:

Hey Bronwyn,

When I was in high school the first two years were probably for me the most difficult years on a physical and emotional level that I have experienced to date. I withdrew from everyone I knew and had no contact with any of the other pupils. I sat at the back of the classrooms so nobody could see me and I asked teachers if I could do my schoolwork in their classrooms at break so as to have as little contact with people as possible. I was doing everything I could to be invisible to everyone.

Cayle did not seem to buy into this.

No matter how many times I would do my best to turn away or ignore him, he would always walk by and say 'Hi Calum, how are things' etc...

In my state I would either walk away or do my level best to pretend he wasn't there. But he persisted. For nearly two years! Not once did he give up and think I was a lost cause. His persistent, warm, friendly grin and happy attitude would drive me mad, and I'm sure I conveyed this, but it didn't seem to deter him.

After nearly two years of this and heading into our final school year, something happened. I stopped and actually replied to one of Cayle's 'Hey Calum!' greetings. We chatted for a bit and in a few days we slowly started having more of what turned into lengthy conversations about whatever we felt like on the day. I went on to regain my once shattered confidence and the Calum everyone knew. Cayle and I went on to do that crazy hiking trip that year and many other adventures.

I still look back at that time with so much respect and gratitude at how Cayle helped me through such a tough period of my life, by doing nothing more than being who he is.

So when people say Cayle is a hero, I know that is true … with or without a uniform.

Much love
Calum

Glossary

BRF	– Brigade Reconnaissance Force
CNO	– Casualty Notification Officer
C-17 (Aeromed)	– The C-17 is a specialist type of aircraft, which commonly performs tactical and strategic airlift missions, transporting troops and cargo throughout the world, and is also used for medical evacuation and airdrop duties.
Dante's *Inferno*	– *Inferno* is the first part of Italian writer Dante Alighieri's fourteenth-century epic poem Divine Comedy. It is followed by *Purgatorio* and *Paradiso*. The *Inferno* describes Dante's journey through Hell, guided by the ancient Roman poet Virgil.
DCCN	– Duty Critical Care Nurse
Donkey boiler	– The principle is that hot water rises (like hot air) and as the fire warms the water, the warmer water will be what comes out of the top pipe.
FOB	– Forward Operating Base
Fynbos	– Meaning fine-leaved, fynbos is a small belt of natural shrubland or heathland vegetation in the Western Cape and Eastern Cape provinces of South Africa.
Gas exchange	– Gas exchange takes place in the millions of alveoli in the lungs and the capillaries that envelop them. Inhaled oxygen moves from the alveoli to the blood in the capillaries, and carbon dioxide moves from the blood in the capillaries to the air in the alveoli.

GC	– Group Captain
Headley	– Defence Medical Rehabilitation Centre Headley Court aka Headley Court
IED	– Improvised Explosive Device
ITU	– Intensive Trauma Unit
Ketamine	– Ketamine is a medication primarily used for starting and maintaining anaesthesia. It induces dissociative anaesthesia, a trance-like state providing pain relief, sedation and amnesia.
LC	– Lieutenant Colonel
MERT	– Medical Emergency Response Team
QEHB	– Queen Elizabeth Hospital Birmingham
RCDM Birmingham	– Royal Centre for Defence Medicine
R & R	– Rest and Recreation
Sharpshooter	– A sharpshooter is one who is highly proficient at firing firearms or other projectile weapons accurately
Tracheostomy (trachy)	– A tracheostomy is an opening created at the front of the neck so a tube can be inserted into the windpipe (trachea) to help you breathe. If necessary, the tube can be connected to an oxygen supply and a breathing machine called a ventilator
Virgil (Dante)	– Virgil is a man with many good and noble virtues. He is a guide and protective to Dante's journey in different levels of hell.
VO	– Visiting Officer
WO	– Warrant Officer